The Jerusalem Diet

Guided Imagery and the Personal Path to Weight Control

Judith Besserman, Ph.D.
Emily Budick, Ph.D.

Copyright © Gefen Publishing House, Ltd.
Jerusalem 2007/5767

All rights reserved. No part of this publication may be translated, reproduced,
stored in a retrieval system or transmitted, in any form or by any means,
electronic, mechanical, photocopying, recording or otherwise,
without express written permission from the publishers.

Typesetting and Cover Design by S. Kim Glassman

1 3 5 7 9 8 6 4 2

Gefen Publishing House, Ltd.
6 Hatzvi Street
Jerusalem 94386, Israel
972-2-538-0247
orders@gefenpublishing.com

Gefen Books
600 Broadway
Lynbrook, NY 11563, USA
1-800-477-5257
orders@gefenpublishing.com

www.israelbooks.com

Printed in Israel   *Send for our free catalogue*

ISBN 978-965-229-401-2

For our daughters
Alison, Rachel, and Ayelet

with love

Table of Contents

Preface xi
Introduction xiii
    Visualizing the Future xv
    Getting in Touch with the Inner Self xix
    The Diet Industry xxi
    Who We Are and Why You Should Listen to Us..... xxiv

Chapter One: The Diet Monologues
    Why I Eat and What I Eat For 1
    The Diet Wars 2
    The Hungers 5
    Our Personal Food Chain 7
    The Infant's Cry 9
    Breaking the Cycle 10
    Recording Your Progress, Keeping Your Journal 12

Chapter Two: Becoming Mindful, Making Choices
    Your Choice 17
    Not a Diet Book 18
    Mindfulness and the Three Questions 19
    No Choice but to Choose 25
    The Threat of Choosing 26

Choice as Empowerment and Promise 30
The Body Machine 33
Reward and Punishment 34

Chapter Three: Imaging and Self-Transformation
Balancing the Scales 37
Guided Visualizations:
     Uncovering Our Motivation 42
The Instantaneous **NOW**
     and the Process of Self-Transformation 46
Getting to the Image 50
Finding the Slimmer Self 54
The Imaging Process 60
You're on Your Way 66
Changing the Myth of Self 68

Chapter Four: Eating to Lose Weight
Feeding the Thinner Self 71

Rule #1: No More Excuses
Getting Started 74
Time to Diet 76
The Fear of Failing 81
On Your Way 83

Rule #2: You Shall Eat for No One's Reasons but Your Own
Dieting and Self-Acceptance 85
Envisioning Success 88
The Polite "NO" 90

Rule #3: You Shall Never Eat Mindlessly
The Mindful Eater 94

Table of Contents

The Hunger Test 97
The Sweet Tooth 99
The Inner Hunger 100
Choosing among Impossible Choices 102
Trade-Offs 106
Trading Down 109
When Mindlessness Is ok 110

Rule #4: You Shall Never Eat on the Run
The Pleasures of Dining 114
The True Enjoyment of Eating 117
Taste Is in the Mouth of the Eater –
    At Least Briefly 117
You are Your Own Best Guest 120
Meal Time Is Meal Time;
    When You Are Tired, Go to Sleep 121
In Praise of the Garbage Can 121

Rule #5: You Shall Never Go Hungry
The Satisfied Dieter 123

Rule #6: You Shall Never Leave the Refrigerator Bare
Preparing to Succeed 128

Rule #7: You Shall Never Deprive Yourself
Indulging Desire 131
That Deprived Feeling 133
Eat This, Don't Eat This 138
Our Just Desserts 141
The Pleasure Principle of Weight Loss 142

Rule #8: You Shall Never Punish Yourself
Self-Forgiveness 144

Being Good to Yourself 145
Forgive, Forget, and Go On 146

Rule #9: You Shall Exercise
Too Tired to Diet 150
The Powers of Exercise 151
Well-Being and Being Well 154

Rule #10: You Shall Trust Yourself
The Hero of the Story 155

Chapter Five: Stepping into the Future; Maintaining Your Weight Loss
Eating for the Forever ME 159
Mindful Eating as a Way of Life 160
What Difference Did It Make?
    Kicking the Eating Habit One More Time 166
More on Reason, Reasons, and Why We Eat 170
Becoming Even More Mindful 173
Talking to Yourself 176
So What's Your Excuse Now? 177
In Defense of the Lovely Lettuce Leaf 178
In the Interests of Eating 179
The Love of Eating 179
Accepting Love, Getting Help 181
Letting Yourself Go – In Caloric Moderation 182
Time to Confront the Future 185
Taking Chances 186
Nothing Succeeds Like Failure,
    Nothing Fails Like Success 188
The Fear of Self-Transformation 190
Dangerous Beauty 193

Table of Contents

    The Anxiety of Regret 195
    The Beautiful ME 197
    The Lightness of Being 199

Appendix: Our Soup-er Recipes
    Blended Zucchini Soup 203
    Cabbage Soup 205
    Cauliflower Soup 207
    Pepper Soup – Red or Yellow 208

Index of Imaginal Exercises 211

Preface

The Jerusalem Diet: Guided Imagery and the Personal Path to Weight Control is not a diet book in any conventional sense of the word, even though it contains many practical tips for losing weight and maintaining weight loss. Rather, it is a book about appetite. It is about our appetite for life, and how we can maintain that appetite, in the healthiest and most personally useful ways we have. In the pursuit of this goal, *The Jerusalem Diet* applies the wisdom and practice of Jerusalem psychotherapist and spiritual guide Colette Aboulker-Muscat.

Colette Aboulker-Muscat was a well-known figure in the Jerusalem psychotherapeutic community. She was also a *yakir Yerushalayim* – a distinguished citizen of the city. Modest and unassuming, she could be found on warm summer days, sitting in the garden of her rather unremarkable Jerusalem house, surrounded by psychologists, teachers, psychiatrists, rabbis, and her other "students" as she called them, who were interested in traveling with her on journeys of spiritual healing only she could take them on. In the garden, Colette would direct her students to close their eyes, while she would guide them inward, toward what she called imaginal space and time.

There, in those imaginal inscapes, where none of the ordinary boundaries of everyday reality pertained, her students discovered unexpected and heretofore unexplored sources of wholeness and renewal. There, for each one privately, were personal pictures of their inner life, private visual narratives that arose effortlessly from the depths of consciousness. Under Colette's calm and reassuring guidance, her students journeyed back in time, and forward again, past the present and into the future: for these powerfully transformative visual journeys were nothing less than excursions into inner healing and change.

What Colette understood, and communicated to us not through directives and judgments but rather through reassurance and support, is that each and every one of us contains our own sources of renewal. We alone know our personal truths. We alone know what we want for ourselves and how we might go about getting it. Change, Colette understood, cannot occur without an image of what that change might look like, what *we* might look like in that changed reality. And so, in her jasmine-scented garden, she guided us on the imaginal journey whereby we might discover the pathways to our own personal transformation.

This book is dedicated to Colette's memory, which is, for many of us, still a transforming image.

Introduction

We diet for as many reasons as we eat. And we eat for as many reasons as there are purposes and pleasures, angers and sadnesses in our lives. *The Jerusalem Diet: Guided Imagery and the Personal Path to Weight Control* is a book about why we eat, and why we diet; why we overeat and then deprive ourselves; why, finally, we fail to feed and satisfy the person we really wish ourselves to be.

It is not the intention of this book to convince anyone to lose weight. "Slimness" is not an ideal. Nor is "plumpness" a sin – except, of course, where issues of health are concerned. The aesthetics of body weight is as subjective as all other fashion trends, from hemlines and hairstyles to makeup and shoes. These are matters for you to decide for yourself. *The Jerusalem Diet* is designed, not to make your choices for you, but to help you make good on choices you have made for yourself. It is geared to assist you in re-imagining who you are and how you want yourself to look, to yourself as much as to the world. This means helping you restructure your internal image of yourself.

The Jerusalem Diet

Too often we diet for the same reasons we eat: to punish or hurt ourselves for our imperfections of body and soul. The consequence is that dieting doesn't work or doesn't maintain its effects: the anger and sadness we hold inside, which makes us want to fill ourselves up with food or empty ourselves out of desire, once again conspire to fill us with self-loathing. We wind up exactly where we started: weighing more than we want to.

This book proposes eating in order to satisfy desire. It strives to enhance rather than diminish your appetite for life and for the pleasures it can provide. Does this make losing weight or maintaining weight loss easy? No. But it does make it manageable in a way that traditional diets do not. And it contributes in a way that almost no other diet plan can to our mental health. Without inner harmony and balance, food or its lack is always going to be doing some psychological job better undertaken by our conscious minds than by our unexamined and ingrained eating habits.

The Jerusalem Diet will tell you how to manage food intake to lose weight and (because this is where so many traditional diet books fail) how to maintain weight loss. Its main purpose, however, is to help you restructure your internal image of yourself, so that right from the very beginning of your eating to lose weight or to maintain your weight you can begin to eat for the slimmer, more slender person you wish to be. It does this through a process called ***imaging*** or ***guided visualization***.

Introduction

VISUALIZING THE FUTURE

Successfully losing weight and, just as crucially, maintaining weight loss, have to do with truly knowing and re-imagining who you are and how you want to look. It is our intention in this book to show you how to do that. In these pages we will help you locate and then become your own slimmer self.

Guided visualization or guided imagery is the basic tool of this self-knowledge and self-transformation. There is nothing esoteric or mysterious or supernatural about imaging. It is, instead, a technique based firmly on the idea that each of us carries within her a mental image of her own best self which can be accessed to permit that best self – the self we already know ourselves to be – to come into existence.[1] Simply put, imaging is a way of seeing in pictures. It builds on basic mental skills that each and every one of us already possesses.

---

1. A word concerning gender. Though men can profit equally from reading this book (and there have been men in the diet workshops who have very successfully lost weight), this book is primarily addressed to the female reader. This is for the simple reason that men's and women's reasons for eating and for dieting, not to mention how the male and female body utilize calories, are different. Male readers are wholeheartedly invited to listen in on this conversation; and we will, on occasion, even include comments intended specifically for your ears. But we are primarily addressing the female reader, like ourselves.

To meet the dual objective of losing weight and then maintaining the loss, *The Jerusalem Diet* calls upon these skills. They are easy to access and employ; indeed, we use them every day, often without realizing it. Change comes about because we believe it is possible – because we allow ourselves to imagine it. If you cannot visualize something, you cannot make it happen. If you cannot see the future you desire, you cannot begin to move into it. Imaging is an instrument of change so powerful that it can literally change your world.

As Colette often said, imaging is not simplistic. It is, however, simple.

Take the example of athletes and other performers. As any golfer or basketball player or baseball player will tell you, if you are going to sink that putt or make that shot or hit that home run, you've got to keep your eye on the ball. And that means that as you throw it, strike it, bat it, or roll it, you've also got to see where it is going to be a few moments from now. You must have clear intentions: where do you want it to be? By visualizing the future in this way, you begin to bring it into the present; you begin to make the future happen now.

All of us, without consciously realizing it, use visualizations in our everyday lives. Seeing with the mind's eye how a new skirt is going to match our favorite blue sweater, and how we are going to look thus attired, is what enables us to buy the skirt and to go out that evening smartly dressed in our brand-new outfit.

Introduction

If we couldn't imagine our future life as a mother or teacher or doctor, we wouldn't be able to pursue these goals to begin with, and we would never become mothers or teachers or doctors. Although the details of the future are always unknown, imagining or imaging a future brings it into the present, initiating the process of transformation.

Imaging, guided visualization, waking dream therapy, and psychosynthesis are all names for a similar, well-tried and proven technique. Over the last several years, guided imagery has been enjoying greater and greater popularity, and not only in professional circles. Representations of guided imagery are all around us, in popular journals and magazines, in the movies and television, in literature.

In the movie *Something's Gotta Give*, for example, the male protagonist (played by Jack Nicholson) is rushed into the emergency room suffering what he assumes is another heart attack. It turns out to be a severe anxiety attack, for which the attending physician instructs him to imagine some beautiful, quiet, unstressful place he'd like to be and describe it to her. Next thing we know the Nicholson character is off in the Bahamas, basking in the sun. The contemplative quiet of this restful place allows him to realize that he has to revisit the various moments in his life that have brought him here, and when he does – when he begins to put his past behind him – he is able to pursue the woman he loves and get his girl. The Bahamas is only one stop on the way to what he truly desires, which isn't an island retreat but a woman with whom to spend the rest of his life.

The process isn't, perhaps, quite as simple as the movie presents it: one moment Nicholson is in the ER, the next moment he's on the beach. But it's almost that simple, and its rewards (even if not necessarily including a trip to the Bahamas or a marriage proposal) are often just as profound.

It is too often the case in everyday life that what we put in front of us is the past and not the future. Instead of imagining a future free of the errors and disappointments and hurts of the past, a future such as we desire, we see ourselves eternally trapped in a present that is weighted down with our memories. We put the past in front of us, and then fear a future that has already happened. This removes the infinite possibilities the future holds. If we can see the promises of the future we strengthen ourselves, our resolve, and our potential for becoming.

None of us doubts the power of memory. Too many of us, however, doubt our power to imagine the future. Yet, our imagination of the future is just as powerful as our memory of the past. In fact, according to contemporary brain research, they are made of exactly the same "stuff." Visualizations are, in the wonderful phrase of Antonio R. Damasio in his popular book *Descartes' Error*, "the memory of a possible future."

What this means is that the images in which the brain thinks about the future are no different in kind from those

Introduction

images we use to think about the past. Our images of the future are just as real, just as much a part of our minds and ourselves, as any memory. And we can use those future-oriented images to move us forward, out of the past, into a new reality just as powerful and just as compelling. In fact, so forceful are our "memories of a possible future" that they can dislodge or change painful memories of the past. That is why they can help us change our lives.

Changing our behavior – including our relationship to food – is no different from the other kinds of future-oriented activities in which we engage. In order to change our relationship to eating, we need to understand what has produced that relationship in the first place. We also, however, need to imagine who we will be and how we will feel and what we will look like after that relationship has been changed.

GETTING IN TOUCH WITH THE INNER SELF

There are two basic forms of guided visualization, both of which are employed in this book. The first has to do with the process of self-discovery, the second with its implementation.

Most of us who eat too much do so for psychological rather than physiological reasons. Very often overeating expresses a conflict in which eating gets the upper hand over other ways of enacting feelings and satisfying desires. Simply bringing eating under control, then, is not necessarily going to resolve the essential problem – it may simply redistribute the weight, as it were. To achieve control in the long run, which has to be the ultimate objective of any meaningful diet, we must get to the root of the conflict that is causing the overeating. But in order to address an internal conflict, we need, first, to identify it.

Imaging through guided visualizations is a way of locating sources of conflict. Through imaging we can identify for ourselves, by ourselves, how eating serves our particular, individual emotional needs. That is the uniqueness of guided visualization as Colette taught it: our images produce personal and private truths.

Our images also produce personal and private paths of action in relation to those truths. In uncovering our innermost knowledge of ourselves, our deepest sense not only of who we are but who we wish to be, imaging enables us to actualize our images of ourselves and to realize them in our everyday lives. This is the second kind of guided visualization you will learn – the kind that helps bring the future into the present and change it.

Many of the guided visualizations in this book are a creative reworking of Colette's own exercises, geared to helping in the specific project of weight loss. There are also exercises designed to facilitate the maintenance of that weight loss later on. These exercises enable you to locate your private, personal reasons for overeating in the past. They also enable you to envision a new future freed of that past. In order to become slim and remain slim, you must change your relationship to eating, now and forever.

To put this in still other words, in order for each of us to move into the future of the slimmer self we want to be for the rest of our lives, we have to have in mind an image of that self. In order to exit the self-defeating cycle of loss and gain, and in order to maintain our desired weight, we need to hold on to that mental image. To start eating in order to lose weight, and to continue eating in order to maintain that weight loss, we have to eat in order to feed the slimmer, healthier self we know ourselves to be. And in order to feed that more slender self, we have to know who she is, what she wants, and what she looks like.

Guided imaging is the heart and soul of the process whereby the new, slimmer self is eased into being.

THE DIET INDUSTRY

The Jerusalem Diet is not a book for everyone. It is a book for those of us who want to understand, better, why we eat and and why we overeat. It is addressed to those of us who want to exert greater conscious self-control over our lives. In many ways, as its title suggests, it is a book about exercising control.

It is about making mindful choices. In this way, it is a book of self-empowerment.

Amazon.com lists over two thousand entries for diet books. From *Scarsdale* to *Hollywood* to *South Beach*, diet plans have swept across a diet-conscious world, which extends from the States through Europe and well into the Middle East. Low fat, low carbohydrate, low calorie: most diets, whether Weight Watchers or Jenny Craig or Dr. Atkins, tell you how to cut something out of your diet so that you can lose weight. Very few of these books, however, transform your relationship to eating so that you can keep the weight off. And almost none of them employ the powers of your own imagination in order to make you the self-conscious and self-empowered agent of your own body that you are entitled to be.

In other words, most conventional diet books tell you how to take something out of your life: namely, certain kinds of foods. They do not give you back something else in return, something that might not only make losing weight easier, but could, perhaps, provide a powerful and sustaining substitute for the pleasures of overeating.

This book provides you with the possibility of joy and satisfaction, not simply in controlling your weight – as important as that is – but also in arriving at self-knowledge and self-control.

Introduction

As most of us veteran dieters all too keenly know, losing weight and maintaining weight loss are not simple matters. They do not depend exclusively on the decision to lose weight or maintain the weight loss – though this is an important first step, as we shall see. They are also not matters of willpower alone. If they were, most of us, who have sufficient willpower to manage our other daily affairs, would not be struggling to lose weight and often losing the battle.

Over the coming chapters, we will, like the diet books with which you are more familiar, provide you with strategies for how to manage food intake to lose weight and then maintain your weight loss. This, however, is not our major purpose. There are already more than enough books out there that do that job. Likely you already own one or two of them. If not, you might well want to purchase one. It's important that you have a food plan. It's also important that this food plan appeal to you. Just as we all eat and diet for different reasons, so different food plans are going to be harder or easier for us to follow. How you eat in order to lose weight or maintain your weight loss is, like every other choice in your life, for you to decide.

Whatever food plan you choose, however, you are going to need strategies for sticking to that diet, especially after the initial, and often short-lived, thrill of taking off those extra pounds. This is our primary goal in *The Jerusalem Diet*. Our goal is to help you change your relationship to food. It is to help you become mindful of why and what and how you are eating, so that you can make your own choices concerning your eating and so that you can stick with those choices.

It is the right of each and every one of us not to conform to public images of the right weight and the right shape. It is also, however, our right to implement the choices we have made for ourselves. This book is geared toward helping you do just that.

WHO WE ARE
AND WHY YOU SHOULD LISTEN TO US

This book has evolved in the most natural and ordinary way. Ten years ago the authors looked into the mirror and saw that they were both carrying around a few more pounds than either of them wanted – quite a few more. Neither of them was obese. Nor did either have any particular eating disorder. Indeed, both of them had very different histories in relation to food. One had been slender, even downright slim, all her life. The other had always been on one diet or another, losing and regaining and gaining even more. But both had become the victims of what they liked to think of as creeping inflation. Through casual inattentiveness, the pounds had gathered where pounds will gather, and there was nothing for it but to take them off. In other words, there was nothing to do but – hated word – diet.

Introduction

In the process of dieting, however, through one of the very conventional systems that measure and limit calories (on the physiological level this is what has to happen in any diet), we became aware of a number of crucial things about dieting. Some of them were things that all dieters, especially habitual dieters, know from firsthand (to-mouth) experience. Some of them were more obscure and complicated.

One piece of the more common knowledge we acquired is how very hard it is to diet, how much willpower and determination it takes to "deprive" oneself (or, at least, what seemed like deprivation), intentionally and consciously, of something so constantly satisfying and available as food. But another less obvious problem we became aware of, in particular as we drew near our goal weights, was that we hadn't the least idea how we were going to maintain the gains (or rather losses!) we had made.

A lifetime of "deprivation" was not an attractive prospect. And it probably wasn't, in any event, a sustainable, or even desirable, goal. Happy, healthy human beings, which is how we thought of ourselves and indeed how we wished to be, very rarely choose to put themselves on a path of perpetual unhappiness and dissatisfaction. And why should they!

As we listened to our own words as we described the situation we found ourselves in, we suddenly realized how much eating was linked in our minds with ideas of pleasure, satisfaction, and happiness. Why should the word "deprivation" even come up in relation to eating in a certain balanced, healthy way? We weren't, after all, starving ourselves. Perhaps, we began to feel, that casual inattentiveness to which we'd attributed those slowly encroaching pounds wasn't as casual as we'd thought. Perhaps our inattentiveness to what we ate was as much an inattentiveness to why we ate.

Had we been inattentive, perhaps, to what it was that was eating us? and to what our eating might be telling us about that? and, consequently, about ourselves?

We came to see that we were caught in a dilemma. We wanted whatever pleasure and satisfaction it was that food was giving us. We emphatically didn't want the something else – namely those extra pounds and inches – that inevitably came along with it.

It was then that the self-aware, intelligent woman within each of us began to become curious about her own eating. We began to analyze our reasons for eating. And we began to formulate and implement strategies for making ourselves conscious of our motives, of our appetites. In so doing, we changed our relationship to food.

In essence what we discovered was that our mindless eating was covering over a more profound and problematical mindlessness in relation to many things. The weight we were holding on to was covering over a more spiritual or emotional weight, which we simply didn't want to see.

Introduction

The one of us who is a psychotherapist and had worked for many years with Colette Muscat adapted some of Colette's guided imaginal exercises and developed others that helped us locate our reasons for gaining weight. These exercises then helped us to lose that weight and, more importantly, they helped us to maintain our bodies as we wished them to be. The one of us who is a literary critic applied her skills in analyzing texts to read the subtexts of our excuses and to find the right (written) words in which to explain guided imagery and transcribe the individual exercises.

Together we began to formalize the theory and practice of eating to lose weight and maintain weight loss. We began to run highly successful weight-loss groups in Jerusalem which implemented the program that began to emerge. And we began to write this book for others to use in their own quest to understand and manage their relationship to eating. Many conversations later, and having maintained to the present our weight loss of over a decade ago, we offer this book to those who, like ourselves, think we can give ourselves more than a piece of cake and a cappuccino – a lot more.

Dr. Judith Besserman is a practicing psychotherapist in Jerusalem and New York City. She uses guided visualizations in her general practice and in the many diet groups she has run over the past ten years. After completing her psychoanalytic training at the New York Postgraduate Center for Mental Health in 1977 and her doctorate at Rutgers University in 1985, Dr. Besserman studied with Colette Aboulker-Muscat in Jerusalem and with Dr. Gerald Epstein in New York City. She has lectured widely on the uses of guided imagery at such places as Tel Aviv University, Bar-Ilan University, the Ramat Chen Psychoanalytic Clinic, and the New York Training Institute. She has conducted imagery workshops both for the general public and for professional groups at Confederation House in Jerusalem, Israel and at the New York Open Center in New York City as well as at private gatherings. Dr. Besserman is currently conducting diet workshops as well as seeing private clients in Jerusalem.

Professor Emily Budick holds the Ann and Joseph Adelman Chair in American Studies at The Hebrew University, where she teaches in the Departments of English Literature and American Studies. She is the author of six books and numerous articles in the field of literary criticism. Her recent work deals with psychoanalysis and literary theory. She recently co-authored a book entitled *Psychotherapy and the Everyday Life: A Guide for the Perplexed Consumer*. Over the last ten years she has assisted Dr. Besserman in running the Jerusalem diet groups.

Chapter One:
The Diet Monologues

"I dwell in Possibility –
A fairer House than Prose."
—Emily Dickinson

WHY I EAT AND WHAT I EAT FOR

How many times have we found ourselves saying one of the following things:
- I'm feeling really good: I'll treat myself to coffee and cake.
- I'm feeling really depressed: I really need some coffee and cake.
- I'm feeling exhausted: I'd better have some coffee and cake.
- I've worked hard today: I deserve some coffee and cake – or a candy bar, or a bag of potato chips, or … you name it! – whatever else seems to constitute that special treat we crave.

Or perhaps we find ourselves saying nothing at all.

Suddenly we are roaming the kitchen, grabbing the first tasty snack that comes to hand. Or plopping down on the couch or in an easy chair, TV on and a plate of ice cream in our hands. We don't even remember how we got there.

Or maybe we find ourselves simply heaping high our plate as we do the smorgasbord at the wedding or bar mitzvah or country club dance – all that incredible food, and free, too!

We eat when we're tired and when we're sad. We eat when we're happy and when we're feeling sociable. We eat because somebody has put food in front of us, and we want to be polite. We eat out of loneliness and out of boredom, out of stress and frustration and anger, and depression. We eat to relax, and we eat to reward ourselves.

We eat and eat and eat and eat.

What we usually don't eat out of is hunger – at least not hunger for food. And we almost never eat as a conscious choice that eating is the best response to what is being asked of us or to what we are feeling, which is another way of saying, what we are asking of ourselves.

THE DIET WARS

Many of us use eating to enact and accommodate certain central issues in our emotional lives. We can all bring to bear countless evidences of this, each in our own way for our own reasons.

Chapter One

For example, as one young woman recounted recently, she was eager to lose ten pounds and yet she found herself frantically searching the kitchen for something sweet to eat. As she was searching, it suddenly occurred to her that she had just eaten and wasn't in the least hungry. And then she suddenly became aware of a feeling of deep sadness, a sadness she hadn't been at all conscious of when she was prowling around the kitchen for food. A good friend had just died. Her search for something sweet had really been a search for something to cover over the feeling of pain. She let herself experience the sadness, and the craving for something to put in her mouth passed.

Or take this experience, which happened to another member of one of our diet groups. She's happily typing away at her laptop in the early morning, right after breakfast, not hungry in the least, when suddenly little messages start appearing on her screen. Without warning the whole system seems on the verge of collapse, and she can't, for the life of her, remember how to get out of the program she's in to avert immediate and total disaster. Finally, she remembers where the battery is and manages to yank it out. She puts in an emergency call to her daughter, who is a computer expert, to ask her what to do. And no sooner has she left her helpless message on the answering machine than she finds herself in the kitchen shoveling pretzels into her mouth. She wasn't hungry when she sat down at her computer, but she sure is now!

The examples are numerous, many of them so typical as to apply to almost all of us: You've been busy all day, on the job, chauffeuring the kids, doing the marketing, and now it is 6 PM, the kids are in front of the TV, dinner's cooked, and you are exhausted. Suddenly there they are: the cheese and crackers left over from Saturday night's party. Instantly you are so famished that there is no way you can do another thing until you've devoured them. And you do.

In all of these instances eating is doing emotional work. It is helping us cope.

Sometimes this emotional work is occasional: some event is occurring in the present that we don't fully register and can't adequately confront. Some of our issues, however, are more long-standing and deeply ingrained. They are harder to get at and uproot. We'll talk more about these later. In either case, identifying the emotional work that eating does for us will not only help us, in the first instance, to lose weight more effectively, but also, far more crucially, it will enable us to sustain our weight loss: for much harder than losing weight is not regaining it. And this is the area in which almost every diet that exists fails.

So perhaps we might begin the process of revamping our relationship to food by accepting that weight loss is, in some very genuine sense, a loss.

One doesn't want to be melodramatic about this, but the truth is that when we give up eating in certain mindless ways,

Chapter One

we've indeed lost something – an old, dear, cherished line of defense. In fact, eating is perhaps our oldest, dearest line of defense, a way we've had since birth of satisfying needs we couldn't otherwise define, let alone satisfy, including the original need of hunger.

In order not to use this habit of eating to satisfy needs other than hunger, we have to find ways other than eating with which to meet those needs. And to do that, we first need to identify for ourselves what those needs are.

Even though there are certain general patterns among us overeaters, nonetheless, none of us eats for the same reasons. None of us shares the same pains and disappointments. It is for each of us to discover who we are and what we want.

Eating in order to lose weight can, in fact, become a pathway by which we come to discover certain things about ourselves. And eating to maintain weight loss can add to that pleasure of self-confidence and self-control which dieting initially brings about. It can supply the ultimate pleasure of our finally coming to satisfy our basic hunger for life.

THE HUNGERS

Not all of the reasons we have for eating are bad reasons. For those of us who are overweight, however, most of them are. For us, the motives for eating are often questionable at best. At worst, they are downright dishonest and self-deceiving – a reason in itself for ridding ourselves of these motives. What we generally call the feeling that precedes our eating is hunger. Calling it hunger justifies to us that the proper response to what we are feeling is food. But is it hunger, really? And if it is hunger, hunger for what?

The truth is that, for most of us who are carrying around weight we feel we'd rather do without, eating is an automatic response. It is a barely conscious reaction to some feeling or other that demands a response, which we decide is food.

Or, more precisely, *overeating* is such a reflex reaction, since eating per se isn't the problem. The occasional piece of cake we eat, or the bagel once a month at the charity breakfast, or mother's special pudding when we make the rare visit home – these aren't the problem, even if we sometimes claim, in our defense, and in order not to make the commitment to dieting, that it is simply impossible for us to lose weight; even a single square of chocolate is enough to make us gain weight. The single square of chocolate isn't the villain. The daily raid on the refrigerator is.

In our effort to lose weight, we might, in order to undo some of the damage of eating mindlessly, have to forego the occasional piece of cake for a while, and the bagel, and the pudding and even the square of chocolate. Later, in order to maintain our weight loss, we might have to content ourselves with rarer indulgences and smaller helpings. But the real culprit for most

Chapter One

of us is eating to excess on a regular basis, day in and day out. It is eating when food isn't primarily or even secondarily what we need or want, but simply what's available and what we've accustomed ourselves to using in order to assuage whatever feeling of exhaustion or unhappiness or frustration we are feeling. Eating at such moments almost never has anything to do with physical hunger. And it is almost always unconscious.

OUR PERSONAL FOOD CHAIN

To put it simply, we overeat when we are not thinking, indeed when we'd prefer not to think. We eat to excess when we are not making conscious choices about what we are eating. We overeat when we are not matching the reality of what's on our plate with our intention or desire to be eating in a way that will help us not gain weight.

Eating whatever comes to hand becomes part of an emotional chain reaction: let's call it the personal food chain of keeping our bodies well padded. And its main function is to suppress an unwanted emotion. Food is suddenly the best drug around. Narcotized we feel full. Gone is the fatigue, the sadness, the joy (yes, sometimes we can want to suppress joy!), the stress, the boredom, the worry, the tension, the depression, the disappointment. In a word, gone is the inner emptiness that is crying out to be filled.

Having eaten, we are full. And full, we feel only the fullness. We don't feel the empty spaces the food is desperately and rather inadequately covering over. At least, we don't feel them for the moment. For as we know all too well, the feeling of fullness very quickly subsides. We empty out, and once again we are compelled to feed the empty feeling, the feeling of emptiness.

When this happens, we are caught unwittingly and almost inescapably in a cycle, perhaps more accurately described as an ever-ascending and worsening spiral: feeling – response – feeling.

Not only do the feelings we sought to overcome through eating recur, but they return with a vengeance. Now they are weighted down with a new sadness, even shame, in the form of extra pounds of body fat. We now eat even more plenteously in order to cover over those extra pounds as well.

Though most of us eat to promote feelings of pleasure and satisfaction – which eating certainly can and does give us – for those of us who eat to excess, eating has become over the years as much a source of dissatisfaction and displeasure as joy. That's why we want to diet and get rid of that excess weight. But in order to break the cycle, we must come to see that overeating is in and of itself, quite irrespective of its consequences in weight gain, a major defense against feeling itself. It is our best escape route from just that pleasure we crave.

Chapter One

THE INFANT'S CRY

Most of us were caught up in this cycle before we could utter a word. Our cries of discomfort from the crib were sometimes simply misinterpreted, and without language, we were unable to correct the misunderstanding. Sometimes, of course, we were indeed expressing hunger. But sometimes it was something else we wanted. Sometimes we were simply feeling troubled or lonely or frightened or even over-full! And when we felt those things and were fed, we came to associate food with satisfaction and relief. We came to believe that food was what we wanted, what we really wanted, whatever else we might be feeling and needing.

Feelings of any kind became connected with eating.

Rather than eating to live, we came to believe that we lived to eat.

Nor did most of our early childhood experiences do anything to loosen the grip of this radical misunderstanding. We were constantly rewarded with goodies, bribed with sweets, loved with foods of all sorts and by all sorts of people in all sorts of relationships to us: at dinners, parties, dates, picnics and holidays, with family and friends, colleagues and associates. We couldn't even grow a year older without marking the occasion with a cake. And every holiday had its foods, to remember with longing and look forward to in anticipation. Not only our bodies but time and space themselves seemed to exist wholly by virtue of food. How then shall we give up the luxuriance of eating?

How can we break the cycle, which goes back further than we can even remember, and which has filled nothing less than the entire time and space of our remembered life?

BREAKING THE CYCLE

We can break the cycle if we can put something between the feeling that sends us reaching for food (whatever it is for each of us), and the moment when our hand arrives to eat one more thing we don't need and don't really want.

We can break it, in other words, if we can stop our hands reaching for the food and think, "is this what I really want?" and, just as importantly, "do I want it more than something else; namely, losing weight?" Could it possibly be that, at this moment (right after dinner, perhaps; in the middle of the night!), I am so hungry that I have to eat that thing, and right now? And if I am that hungry, hungry for what? A good feed, or something else?

What do I really want, and what do I want more: that slice of bread or potato beckoning me (eat me, eat me, eat me), or that other less immediate but no less tangible bodily pleasure of looking and feeling a certain way? Might I not, perhaps, gnaw on a carrot until I figure this out, and decide?

It is really that simple, and that complex. We are about to eat. We stop by asking ourselves what feeling is driving us to food. And then we feed the hunger behind the hunger, the

Chapter One

feeling that is crying out for attention, which our physical appetite can at best only cover over. We eat to feed the person who is sad or lonely or tired or distressed and who knows that food isn't a companion and that it can't give you back a lost night's sleep and that it doesn't solve your problems – indeed, it can only add to them, and drag you down besides. We eat to feed our real hunger, which is a hunger food cannot satisfy. And we eat to feed the person who, thus pared down to the bare trim bones of the feeling self, doesn't want a lot of padding between that self and the world.

We will talk later about feeding that other hunger, the real hunger, which we deserve to have fed and without which we can't help but use food to stifle feeling. In order to do this, we have to identify it. Then we have to befriend it. And finally we have to tend it. We have to nurture who and what we are and want to be.

But in order to get to that stage of the process, when we are able to change our relationship to food once and for all, we have to first put ourselves into the mode of eating a certain way. We have to experience a satisfaction other than that of food: the satisfaction and pleasure of bringing our bodies under our conscious control and losing weight. Giving up the (dubious) pleasure of eating anything and everything we want, we need to experience another pleasure. Not yet having discovered for ourselves our reasons for eating, we need to follow a program that will help us to achieve the pleasure that awaits us in the future.

The essence of this pleasure is simply weight loss itself. Most of us are able to put aside those issues that keep us eating for a certain period of time in order to lose weight – though even in the beginning we may need diversions and subterfuges to get us to eat less (all of which will be provided in due course). Nonetheless, the thrill of losing weight often substitutes for the pleasure we were deriving from eating. It provides interest, excitement even, and a sense of self-confidence. And there is no reason to deny ourselves this pleasure, even in the interests of what is, finally, a more rational, long-range change in relation to how we eat in the future.

So the first step in our program for losing weight (and ultimately, for maintaining that weight loss) is to make the decision to lose weight and then to decide to make good on that decision.

RECORDING YOUR PROGRESS, KEEPING YOUR JOURNAL

Making the choice to lose weight is an important first step. But it is only the first step. You also have to choose to eat in a certain way such that you will indeed lose weight, so that you will experience the pleasure of that rather than the pleasure of uncontrolled eating – the pleasure of making a choice for yourself, and realizing it.

Chapter One

A word that will recur throughout this book is the word mindful. In order to eat in order to lose weight or maintain your weight loss, you will need to become mindful of your eating habits. You will also have to stay mindful of the choices you make concerning what you eat, each and every time you eat.

In other words, having made the commitment to yourself to change your relationship to food, you now need to commit yourself to becoming mindful and staying mindful of when and why you eat.

In the coming chapters we will be providing you with numerous devices for increasing mindfulness. One such device, which we already wish to introduce, is The Journal.

So, another thing you are going to have to do to begin this diet is to go out and purchase a notebook, preferably one that is unlined, since, later on, when we get to the visual imaging, there will be some pictures to draw. Also buy a box of magic markers or crayons: there is no need for us to image our inner world in black and white.

Purchasing the notebook might seem like an easy thing to do, but for many of us it's as hard as passing up a cheese Danish. Like everything else that pertains to becoming mindful and staying mindful, writing down our thoughts, feelings, and experiences (not to mention what we ate yesterday for breakfast) encounters all manner of inner resistances – the same reluctance to being mindful that keeps us reaching for the wrong foods for the wrong reasons. Keeping a journal is a very effective tool in becoming and staying mindful. And, like everything else in this diet plan, it can also become a source of pleasure in and of itself.

So buy something lovely that excites your imagination (this is an eating plan that is all about the powers and pleasures of imagination). Splurge. Indulge yourself. This is the first of many such moments in which, instead of purchasing a fattening treat, you will buy something that will actually help you appreciate and encourage the slimmer, more glamorous person you want to be, who doesn't always need to eat in order to enjoy herself. At the very least, every time you grab for this journal, you will *not* be grabbing for food. But the benefits of the journal are more than that. What you will be giving yourself instead of food is the pleasure and reward of self-awareness. The journal is a gift that you give to yourself, which will replace the gift of the doughnut or chocolate bar by actually helping you control your relationship to eating. That's an equation we will discover over and over again in this diet, especially in the imaginal exercises to follow: you give yourself something you want which isn't food and which enables you to achieve the ultimate reward you want for yourself: that sleeker, healthier, slimmer self.

By writing in your journal, you will be mirroring the progress of your weight loss. You will be confirming that progress, making it visible and real. You will also be reflecting on it. Few

Chapter One

of us are professional writers. Yet our journal entries, containing in our own private, personal language our self-knowledge and our self-discovery, will provide us with a text far more important than anything anyone else can write for us. Writing a personal journal, for ourselves (no one will read this but us) makes our private, internal experiences conscious and concrete. As we write about ourselves, we are bearing witness to ourselves, describing our wishes and desires, which have set us upon this path toward losing weight.

So, on the very first page of your journal, write today's date. Under that date write, not how much you weigh (this belongs to the soon-to-be forgotten past), but how much weight you are going to lose and how much you are going to weigh at the end of your diet. This is your goal weight. Since most of us lose approximately 8 pounds a month, you can project a date when you will achieve your goal weight. The third item you need to write down is the halfway mark, the date at which you will be halfway there.

For the time being, writing down where you are going will help to confirm that you are indeed going there, and going there with determination and conviction.

As you read on in this book and begin the imaginal exercises that are designed to help you lose weight and maintain your weight loss, you will start to record the insights, aspirations, sensations, and successes that these exercises occasion. After each and every visualization you will record the date at the top of the page and write down what you saw or said or did during the exercise, how you felt about it, and where the exercise has led you. Often, as you write, you will gain a new understanding of feelings and thoughts that, until now, have been kept out of your conscious awareness. Writing down the experience of the visualization deepens and enhances the power of the insights and sensations that the exercise has produced.

In addition to recording your experiences of the visualizations, you may wish to record other experiences that relate to your process of losing weight and maintaining the weight loss. Remember to date your journal entries. This is a journey. You are writing a travelogue. You are moving forward, over time and through the landscape of your own personal being. Let the journal reflect the wonder of that. Let it also record your progress.

So, with your journal dated and in hand, read on to chapter 2, about how to become mindful of how and when and why you eat. If you have not purchased a journal, or if you find that, for any reason, you cannot purchase a journal right away, continue reading, knowing that by the time you get to chapter 3 you will have a journal in hand.

Chapter Two:

Becoming Mindful, Making Choices

*"If opportunity doesn't knock,
build a door."*
—Milton Berle

YOUR CHOICE

You've made a decision: you want to lose those extra pounds, or you want to maintain your weight as it is. Now you have to make another decision. You have to decide to make good on that first decision.

That means you have to choose between alternatives. You have to choose to do one thing rather than another thing. And, since eating is a more-than-once-a-day activity, and one which occurs day in and day out, every day of your life, you will have to repeat that choice, make it over and over again, all day, every day.

This can seem daunting. It can be empowering.
Let's make it empowering.

You can make good on your decision to lose weight or not to gain it every time you have to make that choice, which is every time you put food into your mouth.

We said that this book is not a diet book. It is a book about making choices. So, let's see how we can begin making those choices, with a minimum of stress and a maximum of good, happy feeling about ourselves and about the world.

NOT A DIET BOOK

To be sure, there are people who don't have to make our choices. There are people who can eat as much as they want and maintain the body weight they desire. We aren't among those people. So we must choose between two things: the pleasure we derive from eating everything and anything we want and the pleasure we derive from looking and feeling a certain way.

As any psychologist will tell you, most emotional distress has to do with conflicting desires and demands. You want this, and you want that. You are required to do this; you are required to do that. "This" precludes "that"; the one makes the other impossible. And so you remain suspended between desires, unhappy whichever way you turn. As children we were (for a brief time at least) able to have it all, or at least to imagine we could have it all. We rarely considered making choices: everything

Chapter Two

seemed available to us if we really wanted it, and some things really were available to us, like eating as much as we wanted without unwelcome consequences such as gaining weight. We could have dessert before meals, after meals, instead of meals, and it made absolutely no difference to how we looked.

The truth came to us slowly, if at all: life requires making choices, and mental health demands making the best possible choices of all. Choices about how and what we eat are no different from the other life choices we make, except, perhaps, that they are more inescapable and omnipresent. You can quit smoking. You can give up a bad relationship. You can change your job. You cannot stop eating. And most of us cannot eat mindlessly and still look the way we want to look.

MINDFULNESS AND THE THREE QUESTIONS

So, each time we decide to eat from now on, from this very moment forward — for each and every moment in our lives is the all-important present in which we are now living and choosing — we will ask ourselves the following three questions:

1) Am I eating to gain weight?
2) Am I eating to maintain my present weight?
3) Am I eating to lose weight?

The Jerusalem Diet

What do these questions mean, exactly?

Some of us who are veteran dieters can look at a plate of food and know instantly whether the food there is going to help us lose weight or not. Even those of us with vast experience, however, sometimes err (the avocado is our favorite example of a food that sometimes causes confusion: from the point of view of weight loss; it is neither a vegetable nor a fruit, but a fat, to be treated accordingly!). Therefore, reviewing what we see when we look at a plate of food is in order for beginners and veterans alike.

So, what do we see when we look at the plate of food in front of us?

Whether we like it or not, the body is a calorie machine. It takes in calories in the form of food, and it burns them up as energy. Whatever calories the body doesn't need in order to do its job, it generously (too generously!) stores as fat. In order to lose weight, we've got to eat fewer calories than our body needs to maintain its current weight, so that it will take the rest of its daily requirements from storage. To stay the same weight, we've got to eat precisely what our body needs in order to maintain itself; no more, but also no less.

There are many ways of "counting" calories, which is why there are so many different diet programs around. But with slight emendations, one way or another that is what all of us do when we diet: we make sure we are eating fewer calories than

Chapter Two

our body needs to do its work. If the average well-functioning body needs between 1500 and 2000 calories a day to maintain itself (depending, of course, on how much exercise that body is getting, and what its general metabolism is like), then eating 2000 calories a day or 2500 calories a day or 3000 calories a day, no matter what our weight, is not going to result in a weight loss. Indeed, the opposite is more likely to be the case. And if we eat 1000 calories a day, or even 1200 calories a day, we are going to lose weight, even if we are already thinned down.

There are many diets that have come and gone over the years that make claims concerning magical combinations of foods and how they can burn off fat. Perhaps some of these claims are true. Most of them, more likely than not, are not true. There are also people who take off weight through radical surgeries, or who control appetite with diet pills. Many of these weight-loss techniques also work, though some are dangerous in the short run and many unsuccessful in the long run. Stomachs that have been whittled down to tiny proportions have been known to expand voluminously when the choice not to eat is not being exercised.

What is, however, tried and true over centuries of human development, even if it seems rather prosaic and uninteresting, is the equation between calories and energy. What is also true is that maintaining our weight loss is as important as weight loss itself: diets that make extreme and destabilizing demands on our eating habits, even if they yield some initial success, are going to be much harder to maintain in the long run than an eating plan that builds on the everyday and ordinary foods we eat. These everyday and ordinary foods are also the ingredients of a well-balanced, nourishing, and healthy diet.

As in every other aspect of eating to lose weight or to maintain your weight loss, the choice of how we diet is ours to make. Making conscious choices is a crucial ingredient in weight control. So, choose a food plan, and then ask yourself the three questions before you begin to eat:

1) Am I Eating to Gain Weight?

Consider: as you look at the food on your plate, do you see the kinds of foods and in the kinds of quantities that are going to help you lose weight? Or do you see helpings of high-calorie items that are going to ensure that you gain weight?

When you look at the food on your plate, do you see extra calories, or empty ones? And do you want to pad yourself with these calories? Do you want the larger, plumper body this food is going to give you?

2) Am I Eating to Maintain My Present Weight?

When you look at the food on your plate, do you see a meal that will satisfy what you most need and desire (not only now, while you are eating, but later, when the food has literally become a part of you)? Will you be satisfied when you look back

Chapter Two

on what you've just eaten – or, when you look at yourself in the mirror?

3) Am I Eating to Lose Weight?

When you look at the food on your plate, do you see food that is nutritious and healthy: not high in calories, and carefully chosen with the rest of your day's eating also in mind? Do you see food that won't put weight on you? If you eat this food, will you know that you have just eaten to satisfy what you most need and desire, that you are making good on a decision that you have made for yourself?

When you look at the food on this plate, do you see food that will help you achieve your goal for yourself, which is to take off those extra pounds and inches? Do you see nutritious food, low in calories, and in just the right amounts, to nourish your soul as well as your body?

Am I eating to gain weight?
Am I eating to maintain my present weight?
Am I eating to lose weight?
Do I want to be eating this way?

The three questions are really six more complicated questions:

1. a) As I look at the food in front of me, do I see myself eating in such a way that I will gain weight?

and

b) Do I want to be eating to gain weight?

2. a) As I look at the food in front of me, do I see myself eating in such a way that I will maintain my present weight or weight loss?

and

b) Do I want to be eating to maintain my present weight or weight loss?

and, finally,

3. a) As I look at the food in front of me, do I see myself eating in such a way that I will lose weight?

and

b) Do I want to be eating to lose weight?

It needs to be stressed that these are real questions. Answering yes or no to any one of them is perfectly legitimate. We have every right in the world to eat to gain weight or maintain our present weight or lose weight. What is not legitimate is to answer yes to all these questions simultaneously. We cannot eat to gain weight and, at the same time, be eating in order to lose weight or even to maintain our weight or weight loss. These are mutually exclusive options.

In other words, we have to decide; we have to choose to eat to gain or lose or maintain weight. We have to match intention with reality, question 1 a with question 1 b, and so on down the line. We have to eat mindfully to achieve the results

Chapter Two

we desire, the result we ourselves have decided for ourselves that WE want.

If we see ourselves eating to gain weight, we cannot fulfill our intention of eating to lose weight. And there is no point in denying this to ourselves. There is no point in refusing to understand that our answers to these questions concerning how we are eating, which is to say, our choices, are mutually exclusive. And we have to be consistent and realistic about this. We can't eat to gain weight today and eat to lose it tomorrow. One of our choices is necessarily going to prevail over the other, and we all know which choice is going to win out in this particular contest.

NO CHOICE BUT TO CHOOSE

The only thing we have no choice about is not to choose. When we don't choose deliberately, a choice is nonetheless being made for us unawares.

Therefore, when we look at the plate of food in front of us we have to see that the food on that plate is going to contribute to helping us gain weight, or maintain our present weight, or lose weight. And we have to decide, mindfully and intentionally, what we want our eating to do for us. Then we have to choose whether or not to eat everything or anything that is on that plate. We have to see that contained in the choice to put that plate with that food in front of ourselves, or to accept its being put there by somebody else, is the choice of a particular path, with particular consequences.

In other words, we have to bring realities and their consequences into focus. We have to make explicit our implicit (unconscious) choices. And we have to take responsibility for those choices. We have to assume responsibility for the consequences of a choice we are making (whether consciously or unconsciously) to eat one way rather than another.

THE THREAT OF CHOOSING

Precisely because the issue is nothing less than taking responsibility for our choices and making unconscious motivation conscious, these three seemingly innocent questions produce dramatic responses in each and every one of us. If we stop to consider for a moment that, as adults, we are the ones who are feeding ourselves, that no one else is raising the spoon or fork to our mouths but us, then we can begin to see that eating is one of the few things in our lives over which we have total control. We cannot control how we feel about food. We can, however, control what we do with that feeling.

Recognizing that we can control what we eat can become a source of personal power and pride, with a consequence that

Chapter Two

far exceeds that of weight loss. Choosing, we are liberated into self-empowerment, personal freedom.

Yet these questions can, initially, produce anxiety and fear. Because eating seems like the most natural thing in the world, one of those basic life activities that go back farther than any of us can remember, it just doesn't seem to need questioning or justification. Therefore, asking questions about our eating habits can seem like an accusation or hostility against our innermost selves. We eat, the logic goes, because we eat, and we eat what we eat or the way we eat, because, well, that's what and how we eat. It's like breathing. Would anyone ask me to stop breathing the way I breathe?

One man, for example, who was a member of one of our weight groups, was incredulous that he might have to question his each and every meal. After all, he said, he'd always eaten certain foods and he wasn't always overweight. The form his protest took was to claim his "right" to eat his favorite meal of fava beans and rice. This was the meal his mother used to prepare for him, he went on to say. It was a mainstay of his diet. He'd always eaten it. In any event, this was a healthy and nourishing meal. Surely, healthy foods couldn't cause weight gain. Wouldn't it be enough if he gave up snacking and junk food?

For another participant, a woman who was about 60 pounds overweight and who had come to the diet group because she had seen the results among previous members, the three questions prompted tears and the following question: did she "have to" give up potatoes and bread? These were the foods she fed her family daily. They were foods everyone else ate. They were also the foods she herself most enjoyed. They couldn't be what was causing her weight problem. In any case, she didn't eat that much, and her carbohydrates were essential for her health. She also exercised daily and surely her weight was more muscle than fat. Did she have to give up bread and potatoes in order to lose weight?

Can I eat rice and beans? Can I eat potatoes and bread? In asking these questions neither of the above individuals was asking a question about the rules of dieting. For both of them, the questions: am I eating to gain weight, or to lose weight, or to maintain my weight (and/or weight loss) threatened old established habits and defenses. The three questions undermined what they experienced as their natural, perhaps even God-given, "right" to eat what and how they wished. And feeling coerced, as if they were being "made" to do something harmful to themselves, they were asserting that right as if their very lives depended on it.

They weren't entirely wrong about this. In some sense, their lives did depend on the way they ate – not their physical lives, but their emotional lives. As is the case for most of us, eating was doing important emotional work for them, work that had to get done. It was linked to the whole history of their relationship

Chapter Two

to food, going back to early childhood and extending into their everyday relationships with their family and friends. By insisting on their right to eat however they liked and not to change anything, they were expressing a fear of change itself. They were afraid of what might happen to them if they were to alter and make conscious to themselves their relationship to food. Eating seemed to them not a choice but an inevitable and unchangeable law of nature, an expression of their innermost selves that could be violated only at great personal risk.

What got lost in the psychological accounting was that the mindless, unconscious way they'd been eating in the past was itself causing them considerable distress in the form of excess weight. Of course the gentleman of the rice and fava beans had the "right" to eat these foods. And no one was making that woman give up potatoes and bread. But might we not come to see that, in a sense, something – albeit something internal and unconscious – was "making" that woman eat those potatoes and bread; and that in exercising his "right" to eat his beans and rice, the gentleman was exercising his "right" to be overweight?

Not being able to see that their eating habits were themselves the product of internal coercion and of choices being made for them by their own unacknowledged needs and habits, these two people found the three questions too threatening. Not being able to recognize that they could take decision-making into their own power and make the choices necessary to change their relationship to food, they were also, needless to say, unable to realize their desire to lose weight.

CHOICE AS EMPOWERMENT AND PROMISE

The threat posed by the three questions is not to be dismissed lightly, as if those who can't make the choice to eat in a certain way are simply weak-willed and undisciplined.

The emotional work that eating does is work that has to get done, one way or another. It is one goal of this book to help you find those ways which don't involve overeating. One way is already available within the questions themselves.

The three questions, demanding a change, can also be heard as promising the possibility of change: a change that doesn't challenge the rights of the self to feed itself as it chooses, but rather realizes those rights and makes good on them.

This was exactly the way Ellen heard them.

Ellen, 45 years old, joined the group hoping to lose 30 pounds. She had a history of successful dieting, which is to say, a history of unsuccessful maintenance as well. She had recently been on a high-fat, low-carbohydrate diet that had limited her to certain foods. She had lost 30 pounds, and she loved the way she looked. Unfortunately, like most successful dieters, Ellen discovered that as soon as she resumed "normal eating" her lost weight

Chapter Two

quickly found her again. She was once more 30 pounds overweight.

Ellen knew that overeating or, as we put it, mindless eating, was how she swallowed her anger. It was her automatic response to disappointment or frustration, a kind of "I'll show them" response that didn't quite take in that this response was not showing anyone anything at all, except her expanded waistline. By asking the three questions, she was able, in the first instance – and, for her, the most important instance – to put some distance between her emotions and her habitual response: namely, gobbling down whatever food she found at hand. Asking the questions gave her time to decide what she consciously wanted to do. The questions helped break the automatic cycle of anger and eating. Over a period of nine months Ellen lost the 30 pounds she had regained. When the group met for a three-month reunion, she was proud that she had successfully maintained her weight loss. She explained to the group that, even as she had gone on to do the other exercises she had learned over the nine months of her diet, she had never stopped asking the three questions. And she did not stop asking them after she had achieved her goal weight.

Choosing what and how much to eat is not a punishment imposed from outside. It is, rather, a way of taking charge from within. It is making a choice that we can renew and make over and over again. Furthermore, if we don't make that choice, then it is going to be made for us by our own unexamined behaviors and habits, forever!

By not confronting this choice in the present, we doom ourselves endlessly to reenact patterns of behavior that guarantee an unhappy outcome.

In some of the guided visualizations in the following chapters we will trace the sources of our eating habits. Often, however, we will simply learn to circumvent old patterns. The three questions are a way of making invisible behavior visible so that it can become subject to mindful decision making. Sometimes it's enough to see the pattern to do something about it.

> Victor, a 29-year-old man, joined the group because he thought he would look better and live a healthier life (his father had died young) if he lost 10 pounds. The three questions became a mantra for him, and he could hardly believe that he lost the 10 pounds within a two-week period simply by questioning his intentions every time he was about to eat something. For Victor, it was that simple and straightforward. Now, three years later Victor has maintained his weight loss.

It isn't always possible, or necessary, to understand every aspect of one's behavior in order to change that behavior.

Chapter Two

THE BODY MACHINE

The three questions are the first step in revamping our relationship to food. They are also the foundation for restructuring our eating for the future: for the lifetime of eating we are going to be doing as a person who weighs just what we want to weigh, for our reasons, and for our own self-fulfillment.

As recent studies have shown, it is not enough to put ourselves through the discipline of dieting in order, simply, to revert to our old eating habits once the extra pounds are off. We have all done that. And we all know the results. We have seen the diet as a temporary measure, of limited duration, and once slimmer, we felt free to eat again to our heart's desire. What we didn't add was: and free again to gain back all the weight we'd lost.

What we didn't care to acknowledge was that the body is a machine that works in a certain way. It takes in calories in the form of food in order to do its work. If more calories go in than are necessary for the job at hand, the body stores those calories for a later time. This is the genius of the body. It stores fat for such time as when our caloric intake falls and we need to make use of our emergency rations.

In our prosperous, Western lifestyle, our good fortune in having more than enough to eat and the good health to utilize our calories well becomes the bad luck of excess fat stored in places all too visible to the naked eye. It doesn't matter that we have taken off weight in the past. Give the body more calories than it needs, and it will convert those calories to fat.

Therefore, unless we change the way we eat, which is to say, unless we change our basic relationship to food by reducing caloric intake and increasing calorie burnup (which is the mainstay of almost every diet), then we will repeatedly regain the pounds we have so painstakingly lost – and feel so terrible about it as to put on a few more pounds for good measure.

REWARD AND PUNISHMENT

No one, except perhaps our doctor in a medical situation, has the right to take away our right to eat what and how we like. The freedom to choose your answer to the questions – am I eating to gain weight? or to lose weight? or to maintain my weight or weight loss? – is a genuine freedom. It is a right that belongs exclusively to each and every one of us.

However, with choices come consequences. We have to be willing to choose (not simply to accept!) those consequences as well. Along with the choice to eat cake and bagels and baguettes – fava beans and rice and potatoes and bread – comes the choice to be overweight.

We can internalize this knowledge and build on it.

Chapter Two

> *Jennifer was dieting successfully when she passed her favorite bakery. The smells of chocolate and sugar and yeast cakes virtually assaulted her on the street. And she thought for a moment: "I'll go in and have just one little pastry." And then she thought: "I can decide to have that pastry. I can even decide, if I've a mind to, to have two pastries, even three." And then she added the crucial words: "And I can choose to be fat." Eating to gain weight, like eating to lose weight, is a choice. And if we don't make it for ourselves, it is going to be made for us by those same selves, but by default.*

Dieting – that is, eating to lose weight – can seem like a punishment. And maybe in some ways it is. After all, we repeatedly inflict this dieting on ourselves for the crime of eating too much. But sometimes the reverse is true. Sometimes overeating is the punishment. We punish ourselves by overeating or eating the wrong foods, sometimes even to the point of physical discomfort, almost always to the point of psychological distress.

Might eating to lose weight and maintain your weight loss not come to seem then a reward, rather than a punishment?

Perhaps not immediately. And perhaps not all the time. But at the very least, eating to lose weight and maintain your weight loss can represent a way we have of implementing our right to choose. It can become a way we have of exercising control over our lives. And that – certainly as an initial motivation until we have put other psychological planks in place – might just be reward enough.

Chapter Three:

Imaging and Self-Transformation

*Images are vibrations, like light.
They are transparent.
They are the language of our inside,
and the color of our feelings.
They are our first language.
They make us light and alive.
Images bring order to and from our bodies.
They bring us messages from our bodies
to our minds.
—Colette Aboulker-Muscat*

BALANCING THE SCALES

There are many practical steps that we can take in order to lose weight and maintain that weight loss.

In the final analysis, however, what keeps the scales balanced at the weight we decide to be is not so much an external balance as an internal one.

The balance we achieve has to be as much of the mind as of the body. In fact, it has to be between the mind and the body. Somehow, we have to find a way to get our minds and bodies to work together, to do their best for us, to help ourselves be the best self we can be.

If our overeating expresses a conflict within ourselves, in which eating gets the upper hand over other ways of enacting feelings and satisfying desires, then simply bringing that eating under control is not necessarily going to resolve the essential problem. It may simply redistribute the weight, as it were. It may even grant excessive power to our powers of self-discipline, causing further distortion and dysfunction.

To be sure, in the beginning such self-discipline is going to help us lose weight. This is all to the good, since our objective is to be slimmer than we are. Self-discipline has to do with mindfulness, and mindfulness is what eating to lose weight and maintain that weight loss is all about. It has to do with making choices, what Susan Estrich in her *Diet Book for Smart Women* calls "Making the Case for Yourself".

You have to want this for yourself enough to want it more than you want something else: namely, food, and the satisfactions it brings. You have to make a choice that is nothing less

Chapter Three

than a lifelong commitment to your priorities and a commitment to yourself.

But losing weight or maintaining weight loss requires more than just the choice, as important as it is. It requires the means of making good on that choice. And that requires a new sense of self, a new self-image, which becomes the self you eat to feed.

Privileging our powers of self-control may become just one more way we have of ignoring feeling and desire. And this may lead to a new sort of imbalance, no more likely to keep us in balance than ignoring those feelings through eating. Asserting our willpower can produce a resolution of the conflict that does not address and help bring into self-expression those wishes and feelings that have gotten pushed under, first by eating and now by dieting.

The conflict that the cycle of eating and dieting expresses is an internal conflict. It is a conflict within ourselves. In order to resolve that conflict, we have to change not only our external behavior but something far more private and personal within.

We have to achieve the balance among conflicting desires that have until now kept us out of balance.

Many of us have handled these imbalances in the past by overeating. We filled the empty feeling – whether it came from sadness or disappointment, or loss, or an injury to our self-esteem – with food. And we felt better, at least temporarily.

Through eating, we succeeded, for the moment at least, in tipping the scales in the direction of satisfaction and comfort. We filled ourselves with sweetness and bulk and felt pleasantly reassured. We covered our vulnerability with a layer of fat and felt protected. Our fat kept others at a safe distance. It padded our relationship to the world. It insulated us from feelings of sadness and disappointment.

But that worked only for a while. The weight, which protected us – from other people as well as from our own feelings – brought with it a heaviness of its own. We didn't like the way we looked and felt. So weight became the problem we had to confront. And we confronted it by pushing it away just as once we had pushed away the feelings the weight was hiding. We began to diet.

Through dieting, we deprived ourselves of food in a desperate effort to tip the scales in the other direction. Dieting this way expressed a severity of self-discipline just as punishing and unsatisfactory – emotionally and spiritually, at least – as eating. And that spelled our downfall.

By simply ignoring or overruling the needs that eating fulfilled in us, we found ourselves empty once again. And so we filled ourselves with food again, in order to tip the internal scales back once more.

A better way of losing weight and maintaining the weight loss might be to uncover for ourselves what is producing our

Chapter Three

imbalance or disharmony in the first place. We can then, carefully, bit by bit, bring the self into a new balance or harmony. This doesn't have to mean uncovering every aspect of our internal selves – tearing ourselves naked, as it were. Indeed, turning the self inside out can also be a form of self-destructive self-punishment. But a reconciliation of the self with itself, in which we see and know and finally accept the self in its manifold expressions, can be our best way of achieving all those things we want for ourselves. This includes healthier bodies.

Imaging through guided visualizations is a way of locating sources of conflict. It is a way of resolving those conflicts, without self-deprivation and self-punishment. Through imaging we can identify for ourselves, by ourselves, how eating serves our particular, individual emotional needs. At the same time, we can bring into focus the balanced self we want to be.

Through imaging and guided visualization we see ourselves becoming the self we want to be. We begin to become that self. We help that self emerge into physical being.

Through imaging and guided visualization we begin to eat, not in order to bring the scales into balance, but to bring the self into balance. And then we eat to feed that already balanced, slim and well self.

GUIDED VISUALIZATIONS: UNCOVERING OUR MOTIVATION

An imaginal exercise can help me lose weight? If this sounds as improbable to you as some of those miracle diets out there, we can assure you that guided imagery is not some sort of magical cure. It is a tried and true method, not only for weight reduction, but also for the reintegration of the self in our everyday interaction with the world.

Let us begin with imaging as a way of locating our inner truths. Then we can move on to what is, perhaps, the even more powerful aspect of imaging: the way it initiates the process of our self-transformation.

Imaging is a way of accessing our most personal and private, intimate and therefore deeply revealing perceptions of ourselves. It is a way of gaining access to our internal vision, or *inscape*, of who and what we are and who we want to be.

The words we generally use to describe ourselves have, for the most part, already been co-opted by our more mature, rational selves. They bespeak our compromises and accommodations, our acceptance of failure. Images, on the other hand, are pictures that emerge, unguarded, uncensored, spontaneously, from within ourselves. They enable us to glimpse our inner truths as we see them, unvarnished by other people's pictures of us or by the pictures we have come to believe in because of other people's perceptions of us.

Chapter Three

Imaging is our personal, private, internal language. It is a language we by and large keep secret from other people. Indeed, it is a language we have largely kept secret from ourselves.

By accessing our images, we recover this secret language. We come upon the narrative of our life in its truest, least hidden or distorted form.

Imaging is about memory.

It is about retrieving facts and features of our past experiences, which have gone underground and become inaccessible to our ordinary, everyday lives – at least in any conscious, rational way.

All of us have memories that are too painful for us to keep alive in our conscious minds. So we push them aside, bury them, cover them over with other stories that are easier for us to live with, more congenial to the rational history we've put together concerning our lives. Perhaps these stories reveal the people we love in an unfavorable light. Perhaps they don't seem to us to lead any place we'd like to go. Perhaps they simply don't make sense to us. And so we "forget" these stories. We "pretend" they never happened.

But these stories persist in us. Because they are our history, they have inevitably affected the way we think and act. We have integrated them, absorbed them, allowed them to lead us into the future, but unawares, and without our really knowing what the story is and how it has influenced us. It is as if the stories are written in a language we can no longer read.

Imaging translates the stories of our life back into a language we can understand. It enables us to revisit the past, to understand how we came to be who and what we are.

Imaging, then, is about the recovery of these more intuitive and emotional truths concerning our lives. It is a way of prodding these internal scripts out of hiding so that they can enter into our ordinary everyday lives. And by making unconsciously held memories, perceptions, and feelings available to our conscious minds, images permit our inner narrative to stop weighing us down in the murkiness of an unclear past. In this way images become a powerful source of empowerment and personal strength.

Knowing what our stories are, we can begin the process of rewriting them in our own language, to our own ends, in the here and now of our present realities.

> In one guided visualization, Vivian, a 55-year-old woman with 70 pounds to lose, saw herself a slightly chubby child sitting in the family car: she had been on the way to visit a relative with her father, and he insisted she not come in because he was too embarrassed by her appearance. Imaging allowed her to see in this past moment the source of her feeling herself unattractive and fat. It also

Chapter Three

enabled her to understand why, feeling this way, she dealt with her distress, paradoxically, by feeding it.

Her father's embarrassment had left her with a sense of herself as being unacceptable because of the way she ate. Therefore, she had been unable to pay attention to herself in any way that had to do with the forbidden source of her "ugliness" and her father's disapproval: food. Eating mindlessly and to excess became a way of punishing herself for not being "good enough" or "beautiful enough." She wasn't worthy of her own self-attention, certainly not when it came to preparing and eating food.

The visualization provided access to her narrative in its truest, most meaningful form. It presented it as a story of shame and distress, which she covered over by mindless overeating, thereby justifying and fulfilling her father's image of her as unacceptable and fat. She ate to fill out the picture of herself that she was given as a child by her father. And she ate to feed the hunger, which was a hunger for her father's approval and not for food.

As this example illustrates, imaging is about consciousness. It is about uncovering unconscious truths.

Imaging makes unconscious truths conscious.

Just as importantly, since eating is hardly a theoretical or imaginary process, it enables us to enlist consciousness on the side of desire. Knowing what we want – and what, perhaps, is preventing us from getting it – enables us to discover ways of countering our own internal resistance. It enables us to choose.

THE INSTANTANEOUS NOW AND THE PROCESS OF SELF-TRANSFORMATION

All of us believe we are the people our parents told us we are. Those of us who were told we were beautiful or smart or kind or lovable grew up with this knowledge in our souls. Those of us who were told we were unruly or hard to teach or even stupid carried this identity hidden within us as well. Compliments and criticisms stay with us long after they've been uttered. We keep these images within ourselves for a very long time, sometimes forever.

Imaging locates the origins of our images of ourselves. It tells us our stories of ourselves as tales of needs and desires, wishes, fears, and hurts. It tells those stories to the adult listener who now has the wisdom to evaluate and transform what our childhood selves were too young to understand and cope with.

As children we believed everything we were told, especially by our parents. As adults we can be more cautious and skeptical.

Chapter Three

Imaging recovers whole scenarios of childhood. And more: as such narrative pictures roll effortlessly forward into the future, they reveal us to ourselves as we would like to be, as we in some sense already know ourselves to be, inside, in our wholeness and renewal. Imaging frees us from the stories of defeat that have kept us imprisoned and helpless. An imaginal journey is an experience. It is an event occurring neither in the past nor in the future, but in the present. In the present, we begin to realize the possibilities and begin the process of our becoming.

Guided imagery leads us inward to a place where the ordinary boundaries of physical time and space do not exist. In this place of imaginal space and time, which is uniquely our own, we exist in the living moment. Past, present, and future are one. Everything is possible, and we are present to every possibility.

This new geographical and temporal spaciousness permits us to encounter ourselves, our lives, and our universes in ways that are new to us. We awaken out of the narrowness of familiar space and time, with its restrictions and impositions, and release ourselves into new possibilities. We discover ourselves in a different landscape, or inscape, that we didn't know was available to us – even though it was always there inside us, an untraveled part of ourselves.

In this new place within the self we find unexpected resources of wholeness and renewal. In this place we meet ourselves, find ourselves, locate parts of ourselves that we did not and could not see from where we ordinarily live, at the tip of the iceberg of ourselves. We uncover both the questions and the answers that our lives have put to us. Images, indeed, are revealing glimmers of the answers to our deepest, still-unspoken questions.

The images that suddenly appear arise from the depths of our unconscious. They transform our consciousness.

The new awareness they produce, not only of the world but, more importantly, of ourselves in that world, permit us, and enable us, to step off our beaten paths, to discover the surprises awaiting us around each and every imaginal bend in the road.

Far from being static, images are progressive. They contain entire narratives. These stories are not simply about the past, as if being told from the distance of the present moment. Rather they embody the past in some more immediate and unguarded form than their verbal equivalents.

They are also not simply *about* the future. Rather they produce in the present an experience of the future. They enable the future to begin to happen, now in the present, which is where every future takes its beginning.

From the time we are small children, all of us have dreams. Some of those dreams we gave up along the way. As we changed, our dreams changed with us and what had once seemed possible or desirable no longer seemed that way. Many of the decisions we made concerning our future were good ones. They took into

Chapter Three

account the other decisions we had made, and so our dreams grew and changed along with us. Together we and our dreams moved into the future. Without those dreams, even the ones we left behind, we couldn't have moved forward at all. But sometimes, along the way, we gave up on dreams we weren't quite ready to give up or that we didn't really have to sacrifice. Those dreams may still inhabit and sometimes haunt us. They may also help us to locate the sources of our dissatisfaction in the present and the place we want to move on to in the future.

Imaging recovers those dreams, so that we can revisit and perhaps remake or revise those decisions. Even more importantly, it reminds us that we have had dreams, that we are in essence dreamers. Finally, however, and even more pertinently, imaging makes available to us our present dreams which, with our adult mentalities we have been too shy or too mature or too rational to admit to. After all, we all gave up wishing for things a long time ago.

Yet, if we cannot envision ourselves as we wish to be, chances are we will not be able to change ourselves. We will have no guide in our pursuit of the new. We will have no model, no image, toward which to move. We may not realize all our dreams. But that is no reason not to dream. That is no reason not to desire. To replace our old sense of our selves as fragmented and dysfunctional we do not have to manufacture a whole new self out of nothing. Nor do we have to realize the impossible. We have only to find ourselves as we would wish to be, and by finding ourselves, set ourselves on the pathway by which we might become that new self.

No one can guarantee where we will arrive. One human possibility is always failure. But we will not know that if we do not set out on our journey. Success is just as real and compelling a possibility! But success depends on setting out. We know where we are now. We need to know and see and understand where it is we want to go.

It is precisely because images enable us to see ourselves in new and different ways that they are transformational. Arising from deep within, they change our consciousness of ourselves. They give us a new picture of who we are and who we want to be. Within each one of us is a rhythm of renewal and healing. Images release this rhythm. Through imaging we are granted the possibility of change, of becoming who we are and who we wish to be.

GETTING TO THE IMAGE

We approach imaging with the attentiveness of a focused heart, knowing intimately the direction and desire of the heart. We ask ourselves what it is that we desire, and what we need to confront in order to achieve that desire. It is the heart, not the brain, which contains our deepest knowledge. Therefore, what

Chapter Three

we are asking of our hearts isn't to give us this or that feeling, but to yield up to us its intelligence, its knowledge. The heart, we know, knows things the brain does not. And knowing that fact about the heart, we can get our hearts to speak to us directly, to tell us what we already know in our hearts that our brains do not yet know and cannot tell us.

We access images by closing our eyes and breathing out. We remove ourselves from the immediate present of our lives, with all its noisy encumbrances and distractions. We let our bodies become silent and enter the spaces of quiet where our internal pictures reside. For a moment we come free of the laws of the material universe. We are released from the constraints of knowledge and intellect that tie us to the familiar world. We shed the weight that holds us down. We discover who we truly are, who we truly wish to be, and what we truly desire.

Now we commence.

Read the following exercise through to the end, and then do it. It is a model of all the exercises to come.

IMAGINAL EXERCISE #1
A ROOM OF YOUR OWN
(Introductory Exercise)

Sit in a comfortable chair, both feet resting on the ground, your legs uncrossed and your arms relaxed. Close your eyes and, breathing out three times, feel yourself relax, feel yourself drifting away from the here and now of your everyday life. Hear the silence around you. Turn your senses inwards.

Now imagine that you are in the favorite room of your house. See how the room looks. Identify its features, detail by detail. Sense how you feel in this room. See if there is anything in the room you would like to change. Breathe out. See the room become as you wish it to be. If it is fine as you see it, leave it as it is. Feeling satisfied and content with what is now before you, breathe out and open your eyes. Take the satisfaction and contentment you feel with you as you come back into the here and now.

If you were able to do this exercise, then you experienced how, from the moment you imagined yourself someplace else, you left the space you are now occupying. You also moved out of the duration of time as you generally know it. In the room you held in your imagination, it could have been morning, afternoon, or evening. You were not here with this book in your hands, sitting on this chair, experiencing today's challenges. You were in another space, removed from time.

Chapter Three

In your imagination you can be anywhere, at any time. You are awakened out of the narrowness of familiar time and place. You are released into new possibilities.

Imaging permits us to move out of the strict chronology of past, present, and future into an instantaneous, atemporal moment, NOW, where all possibilities exist and can be realized. This realm of the imagination, the world of the NOW, is as real and as present as the world we can see with our eyes open. Visualizations allow us to make room for that world, the space of the eternal NOW where we can change our sense of ourselves.

Far from being abstractions, these new discoveries are sensual; they lead us back into our senses rather than into our thoughts. We can taste the new fruits we find. We can see and smell the flowers, feel and hear the qualities of light and darkness, and of wind and air, which reside within the self. In this way imaging recovers the sensuous richness of our inner reality. It permits it to flow into our daily life, infusing our life with a powerful abundance.

FINDING THE SLIMMER SELF

Some of our images are memories.
Some of our images are motors.
Imagination puts the mind, the body,
and the feelings into motion.
    —Colette Aboulker-Muscat

In the coming chapters we will provide some of the nitty-gritty details of how to eat in order to lose weight and maintain weight loss. Throughout, we will accompany these suggestions with imaginal exercises that will facilitate the process of weight loss.

Fundamentally, as the **three questions** in chapter 2 already suggest, losing weight is largely a mechanical process of retraining the self in relation to eating. You have to articulate and make choices. And you have to remake those choices over and over again. Eventually, however, eating to lose weight or maintain weight loss is a process that must come to feel as natural and satisfying as eating itself. Otherwise, it will be difficult for you to sustain the process. We might easily lapse back into old patterns and behaviors.

The guided exercises that appear throughout this book will help you to confirm and consolidate your desire to lose weight. They will help you transform your needs and desires in relation to food so that you can maintain your weight loss.

Chapter Three

A major objective of this book is to put you in touch with your best internal images of yourself so that you can feed that self and not the self which is heedlessly gobbling down calories and putting that other happier, sleeker, more beautiful self to shame. To do this, you need to come to see and value the beautiful self. You also need to understand its basic relationship to food and to all its other needs and desires. You have to begin to understand your relationship to food as itself a part of those other needs and desires and you have to find ways other than food to satisfy them.

If feelings of deprivation and self-punishment are often what derail us as we seek to shape our bodies into their best forms, this book will counter those scenarios of deprivation and self-punishment. It will draw, instead, pictures and stories about feeding and nourishing yourself. These pictures and stories will, in fact, feed and nourish who you are and who you want to be.

This book, in other words, will teach you how to give yourself what you decide you most want and need. If that's excess pounds, then let it be excess pounds, and let those who have contempt for "fatties" find some other project. Remember: being fat is not a sin. And no one, *no one* (except, perhaps, your health care professional) has the right to make that choice for you. But if what you choose for yourself is *not* excess pounds, then you have to discover what it is you *do* choose, and, equally important, how you might go about getting it.

We begin by putting ourselves in a psychological place where we can accept the discipline that eating properly entails without at the same time throwing us hopelessly out of balance. The visual exercises that will accompany the eating plan in the coming chapters begin the work of imagining the inner self in her perfection and internal balance. They begin the process by adjusting the scales that really matter the most – the internal scales – so that, even after the excess weight is long gone, you can continue to eat to feed the slimmer self.

But first you have to find that slimmer self.

So here is Imaginal Exercise #2 in our program for losing weight and maintaining your weight loss.

Note: All the visualizations in this and later chapters should be done in the same manner. Always read the visualization through to the end. Then, closing your eyes and concentrating on your breathing, do the exercise as written. After you have done the visualization, consider the significance of the images. There are forty-three visualizations in this book.

We recommend that, when you complete the exercise, you record your imaginal journey in your journal. Recording the visualization intensifies its effectiveness

Chapter Three

and concretizes the experience. Remember to date your journal entry. Write down your thoughts and reactions to the exercise and draw in color any significant images that occur to you. This is your private, personal journal. It can become a source of clarification and inspiration for you. Do not concern yourself with your artistic abilities. You only have to be willing to permit yourself the freedom to let feelings flow into images.

IMAGINAL EXERCISE #2
THE TWO MIRRORS

Sit in a straight-backed chair, legs uncrossed and both feet firmly on the ground, your arms relaxed. Close your eyes and breathe out three times. Counting each breath backwards from three to one, you reach a perfect zero, the circle of your imagination. Enter this circle, where all things are possible.

See yourself standing between two full-length mirrors. Looking into the mirror in front of you, see yourself as you look NOW. Notice what clothes you are wearing, the style of your dress, the color of your clothes, everything about yourself in the present moment. See and know what it is about your appearance that pleases you, what you really like about yourself. Is it your eyes? your smile? your hair? your face?

Now see what it is you wish to change in your appearance. Know what it is that you wish to discard internally and externally. Know what you wish to be rid of. Push this first image aside with your hand, moving it to the left.

Breathe out, exhaling completely. Turning to the second mirror, see yourself transformed, looking as you would like yourself to be. See what you are wearing. Notice the changes in your body. Feel the changes in your body.

Breathe out three times. Now ask yourself what it is that you must do to actualize this image of yourself.

When you have received your answer, open your eyes.

Know: you are already on your way to realizing that self.

This exercise should be repeated every day for one week. During the first three days you will stand before both mirrors. The last four days, you will see yourself standing in front of the second mirror only, with its reflection of your transformed self.

Chapter Three

For everyone who does this exercise, the images and the answers are different. There is no correct way to see oneself. Nor is there any correct internal image to which one is supposed to arrive. In one of our women's groups, some women saw very vividly the excess weight on their thighs or tummies, bulging beneath their clothes. Others saw their faces as too rounded or their arms as too heavy. One woman wanted to remove the heaviness in her heart. Each person, in other words, located what was troubling to *her*, not what was necessarily troubling to someone else. And each person discovered in her transformation a self that conformed to her desire, and to her internal mental image of how she wished to appear. Some women saw themselves outfitted in old clothes they could no longer wear. Others saw themselves in new outfits they would purchase. Some women didn't see themselves dressed at all, but stark naked and very beautiful.

This is the value of images: they give us *our* pictures of ourselves. Images reveal to us our own personal and private truths. And they give us the direction we need in order to realize our desire.

> *In one rather startling version of the imaging experience, Manny, a 47-year-old man, reported that, while he could see himself clearly in the second mirror, he couldn't see himself at all in the first mirror. Manny weighed 220 pounds, but he had no sense of how he looked. His scale*

told him he had to lose 70 pounds, but that overweight man wasn't, he came to realize, who he saw himself to be at all. When he asked himself what he needed to do to actualize the image he had of himself, he shattered the first mirror. His weight loss was dramatic, and as of the writing of this book, three years later, he has maintained that weight loss.

THE IMAGING PROCESS

Our inner images tell us truths that we are ready to hear. Our images do not lie. If the answers to our questions are not forthcoming, or if the message is unclear, which can sometimes happen, we are also revealing a truth to ourselves. We are saying to ourselves that we aren't ready *at this particular moment* to see and hear the truth. If this happens to you, you can do the following exercise. Remember to date, record, and draw the results of the exercise.

IMAGINAL EXERCISE #3
THE OBSTACLE IN THE PATH

Closing your eyes and breathing out three times, see yourself on your own road, walking in the middle of the day under the bright sun. You see

Chapter Three

a turn in the road ahead of you, and you know that your slimmer self is waiting there.

There is an obstacle on the road which prevents you from reaching this self.

Stop and examine the obstacle. Knowing that in your imagination all things are possible and all help is available to you, consider whether you wish to overcome this obstacle. If you wish to overcome the obstacle, then discover the way to get to your slimmer self. If you choose not to overcome this obstacle, know what limitations accompany this decision.

Breathe out and open your eyes.

One successful encounter with THE OBSTACLE IN THE PATH – and the overcoming of it – is Sarah's:

> *Sarah was 42 and a well-known scholar in her field. She was doing her utmost to lose weight, but, as she sadly reported to the group, she simply could not lose those extra pounds. Despite her new consciousness in relation to what and why and how she was eating, she did not lose any weight during the first month in the group. This was extremely baffling, since most dieters, when they begin to change their eating habits, experience a quick weight loss. This was just not happening to Sarah.*

> Then, in a moving and dramatic experience of guided visualizations, she saw herself over the preceding few years, when her mother was dying, gradually gaining the weight she now wished to lose. Her weight, she came to see, was deeply associated in her mind with her mother's presence. By providing her with access to the sources of her ambivalence and uneasiness, she was able not only to understand her deep internal resistance to losing weight, but to go the next step as well. Within the exercise she was instructed to ask her mother for permission to lose the ten pounds she had gained. Having settled her sense of discomfort in relation to her mother, the desired weight loss followed within the next two months. Since that time, nine years ago, Sarah has successfully maintained her weight loss.

For those who are unable to receive the message of what they need to do, or for those who prefer not to overcome the obstacle on their road to the slimmer self, the process of losing weight will take longer. It does not mean that you cannot lose the weight you wish to. Rather, it means that the challenge facing you as you change your attitude toward food is ambivalence. Be aware of your ambivalence as you continue on your journey to your slimmer self.

Chapter Three

Charles, a young man of 20, believed that the 27 extra pounds that had been weighing him down for several years now were the fault of his mother's good cooking. He was the baby of the family and the butt of jokes from his thinner brothers. He insisted that his mother's "supplying" him with baked ziti and over-stuffed sandwiches was the main source of his weight problem. He was slightly embarrassed to learn that it was he who was now responsible for feeding himself. Unable to locate his slimmer self on the other side of the mirror, he began the journey described above.

The obstacle on the road to his slimmer self was a mountain of food. He easily identified his obstacle as food itself, and his enjoyment of eating as the issue challenging him. He expressed uncertainty when asked if he wanted to remove the obstacle. "I could kick it away," he said, "but I think I would rather just jump over it." And he did just that, surprising himself with how quickly he could now find his slimmer self.

Within two and a half months Charles lost 27 pounds. A year later he was pleased to discover that he had maintained his weight loss even though he was no longer eating to lose weight. Charles had passed the danger point. The conscious, mindful attitude Charles had acquired through imaging enabled him to take full responsibility for his eating. This was the key to his success, and the key we all need to find in order to lose weight and maintain our weight loss.

Another visualization that can help us understand our reasons for holding on to those excess pounds we so desire to get rid of is based on a story (perhaps apocryphal) concerning catching monkeys in India. It is a well-known fact that monkeys like beans. And so to capture the monkeys, large jars of beans with narrow openings are left in the jungle. The monkeys, wanting the beans, push their hand into the jar and grab a fistful of beans. But now their hand, holding a fist full of beans, is caught in the jar, and the monkey is unable to free itself. They can only get loose by letting go of the beans. But they don't let go. And so it is with us, seemingly trapped with our excess weight.

IMAGINAL EXERCISE #4
HOLDING ON

Close your eyes, breathe out one time, and imagine that your hand is in a jar, clenched in a fist. You are holding on to something that will not allow you to lose weight. Without dropping what you are holding on to, open your hand. See what it is, and open your eyes.

Chapter Three

Three women in one of our groups had fascinating responses to this last exercise.

> *One woman saw that she had been holding on to a key. She was instructed to consider what this key meant to her. She immediately knew that she had the key she needed to lose weight, but that she was still not using it. Instead, she was just holding on to it.*
>
> *Another woman described what she found in her hand as an idea. And that idea was: no matter how much weight she lost, she wouldn't find a companion. Her weight was a compensation for being alone, and her notion that losing weight would not necessarily bring a companion with it was reason enough not to lose weight. When asked whether being overweight and lonely was preferable to being thin and lonely, she had to admit that it wasn't; that indeed, even if getting thinner might not change her life in every way, it would change her life in one way that counted: she would have a thinner, healthier body.*
>
> *Finally, a third young woman, with over 100 pounds to lose, discovered that what she was holding on to were gold coins. Not ordinary, everyday coins, she emphasized, but the kind of old coins you find in treasure chests. Was her excess weight somehow precious to her, and precious in some very old, very secret, even buried, way? Trying*

to understand what her image was telling her about the process of her weight loss, she remembered a photograph of herself as an extremely chubby baby. As she described the baby in the picture, she puffed up her cheeks and pushed her head back to show us how she looked. "It wasn't my fault," she said of her baby self; and indeed she was right: it wasn't her fault. But to free herself from the jar, this woman will have to let go of the past and to eat for the future self she wants to be.

Record and illustrate your experience in your journal, including any new thoughts and emotions that come to mind.

YOU'RE ON YOUR WAY

You have now uncovered who you wish to be, the person you already are on the inside. This is the "you" who has been hiding beneath those extra layers of fat. This "you" does not need those layers of fat. In spite of the camouflage, this image has survived within you. From now on you will eat to feed this you. This you knows the difference between the hunger for food and the hunger for other things. You know when food is being used to cover up and substitute for something else. And you know that you are entitled to be fed as is appropriate to you and *your* needs.

Chapter Three

On every trip to the refrigerator or supermarket or bakery, from this moment on, you will be this knowing you.

You will eat for no one else but yourself in your slimmest, trimmest, happiest form. You will begin to change the fabric of your life, fashion a whole new you woven out of the elements of yourself as you are and wish to be.

Read this exercise through first and then, closing your eyes, go through the steps outlined below:

IMAGINAL EXERCISE #5
REPAIRING THE WEAVE

1. Imagine that you are seated before a loom. Know that you can reweave your life by replacing in the loom those threads that are no longer fitting and appropriate to the tapestry you are now producing.
2. See the general color of your tapestry, the nuances of its shades and textures.
3. Undo what you don't like. Redo it as you want it to be.
4. Feel how repairing what has not been done well and what is displeasing to you is a rewarding experience.

5. See how you are choosing the threads for a new and more beautiful tapestry. Sense and feel how you are now an experienced weaver. You are producing the best possible weave.
6. See how when your weaving is repaired, it looks and feels new.
7. Know that for each new beginning, God is preparing the skeins.

This is a particularly delightful and colorful image to record, and requires no artistic ability whatsoever!

CHANGING THE MYTH OF SELF

Each of us has a story about ourselves that shapes and controls our external life. It tells us who we are and how we have to behave in the world. It is the tapestry of self, the myth we obey in our everyday dealings with the world, even against our sense that this myth doesn't express the whole of us and may not be the story we want guiding our lives.

Through internal images we can change that myth. In the instantaneous NOW of imagination we can see what belongs to the past and what brought us into the present. We can also step into the possibilities of our future and in so doing bring that future into the present.

Chapter Three

After we return from our imaginal journey, our new myths continue to inform our experience of ourselves and our world. New possibilities are already at work in our bodies, in our thoughts, and in our feelings. We are reworking our myth. We are becoming part of a new story of ourselves.

Through images we come to recognize distress as a message from within. We unmask the meaning of that distress and imagine ourselves past that distress into fulfillment.

By helping us discover the harmony within ourselves and between ourselves and our world, images enable us to balance the scales, to discover the balance that is the harmony of our internal self – the only balance that matters.

Now you are ready to put all your past diets behind you: your attempts and partial successes and ultimate failures. The past is over. The future is ahead of you. You are ready to bring your inner images into fulfillment. **NOW**.

Chapter Four:
Eating to Lose Weight

"The trouble with eating Italian food is that five or six days later you're hungry again."
—George Miller

FEEDING THE THINNER SELF

The purpose of the imaginal exercises in chapter 3 was to uncover the thinner, sleeker, more attractive person you know yourself to be. It was also to start you on the journey toward realizing that self, not only in mind, but in body as well. Through your imagery, you came to see this self. You came to accept that this self exists, and that this is the self you are already on your way to becoming.

But there is more you need to know and more you need to do in order to lose weight and, even more importantly, to maintain your weight loss.

Most of us who are overweight have developed lots of bad habits over our years of inattentiveness. We stopped paying attention to what we were eating and why we were eating it. We also gave over to food all sorts of psychological power that really has nothing to do with eating and even less to do with food. If eating is doing psychological work for us, then that connection between eating and the emotions needs psychological undoing. We need to find new ways to do old emotional jobs.

It isn't enough simply to say "I'm going to lose weight," although this is an essential first step. You need to find ways to convince yourself (sometimes even trick yourself into believing) that you can do this thing. You also have to find ways to believe that you can succeed without causing yourself (and the others with whom you share the space of your life) undue and unmanageable suffering.

In other words, you have to find strategies for relating to food differently. But you also have to be careful that these new strategies don't push you out of balance in some way that will lead you to revert to your old eating patterns.

You need substitutes (some of them temporary, some of them longer lasting) for the satisfactions food has given you in the past. To start with, one of those substitutes may simply be a shoulder to lean on. And that shoulder might well be a diet plan on which you can come to depend. The plan itself will have to provide further substitutes to keep you going. It will also have to give you some mechanisms and strategies so that you do not

Chapter Four

return to unconscious and uncontrolled eating. But most of all it has to be a plan you can trust.

Here is our plan.

Here are **Ten Rules** that you can follow in order to eat to lose weight and maintain your weight loss.

THE TEN RULES OF EATING TO LOSE WEIGHT AND MAINTAIN WEIGHT LOSS

1. NO MORE EXCUSES.
2. You Shall Eat for No One's Reasons but Your Own.
3. You Shall Never Eat Mindlessly.
4. You Shall Never Eat on the Run.
5. You Shall Never Go Hungry.
6. You Shall Never Leave the Refrigerator Bare.
7. You Shall Never Deprive Yourself.
8. You Shall Never Punish Yourself.
9. You Shall Exercise.
10. You Shall Trust Yourself.

The Jerusalem Diet

Rule #1:
NO MORE EXCUSES

GETTING STARTED

The first rule in eating to lose weight and maintain weight loss is to acknowledge that *YOU are an important person. YOU are worth dieting for.*

Most of us have many excuses for not dieting and, later, for not maintaining the eating pattern that has helped us lose weight. We all know the litany. We have uttered many of these sentences ourselves.

I don't have time to diet.

This isn't the right time for me to diet.

I am too old to diet.

I can't prepare the foods I need to diet.

I can't do without sweets.

Eating is my only pleasure.

And since many of us have dieted in the past, and failed to maintain our weight loss, we back up all these other reasons with the one that clinches them all:

There's no point in starting a diet since, obviously, given my track record, I am only going to fail once more. Even if I

Chapter Four

lost weight again, I wouldn't be able to maintain that weight loss. Look at me now! *I'm just too fat to diet!*

These are the things we say to ourselves to justify our eating something that we know is going to put weight on and which we know we do not have to eat. These are our excuses for not changing our eating habits when we know that changing those habits is the only way to lose the weight we've decided we want to lose. They are a way we have of remaining in the place of indecision in which choices are made for us by others and by our own unexamined motives.

Take the example of one woman, who despite the fact that she had come to the group because she wanted to lose 40 pounds, declared at the outset that she was tired of trying to diet. We pointed out to her that the word *trying* expressed her fear of failing. It also ensured that failure. *To try* to diet meant that she was *not* deciding either to diet or not. Rather, she was deciding to occupy some noncommittal space in-between. She was deciding not to choose.

What this woman was advised to do was to ask those three questions each and every time she ate something. And if she discovered that she was eating to gain weight, she had to declare to herself the consequences of that choice. "I can eat this food, and I will not lose weight, and I will be overweight."

Remember: eating to lose weight is about choosing what *you* want for *yourself*. Overeating is just behavior, with consequences. You've now chosen to change that behavior. So, commit to changing it. And don't let anyone else, either, deter you from that goal! Discover not only that your excuses excuse nothing at all, but that you don't have to make excuses – not to anyone! – for wanting to lose weight. Losing weight is your right. You are worth doing this for.

TIME TO DIET

The most popular excuse we give ourselves for not starting a diet, or for not staying on one, has very little to do with what we might self-accusingly think of as self-indulgence or weakness. On the contrary, it reflects our sense of personal worthlessness. This is the excuse that we are simply too busy to diet. We don't have the time to diet, at least not now, when we have so many other more important things to do. We are not worth the time and effort to diet, we say to ourselves.

The truth is that most of us are busy. Some of us are perhaps even extraordinarily busy. The question is: what are we busy with? Which is to say, for what are we not too busy? For which things do we indeed have time?

For most of us the answer is our children, our spouses, our friends, our parents, our jobs, our communities – everything, in short, but ourselves. The last name on the list is our own.

Chapter Four

Where has our time gone, such that we can say "I do not have time"?

Do you have time to prepare a salad for yourself? It certainly doesn't take more time to prepare a salad than to bake a cake or cook a stew or prepare any number of dishes that you make for your friends.

Nor does it take more time to buy the foods you need rather than the foods you'd do better off without.

It does take time to prepare the carrot sticks and other nibble foods you need for snacking; and it does take time to pack a diet lunch rather than buy a cinnamon cake at the local coffee shop. How much time? And why is that amount of time "too much time" (which we don't have)?

There may well be situations in which your food needs and the needs of others (the members of your family, for example) clash, or where the time that you'd spend preparing some low-calorie foods is otherwise committed to other people and their needs, not yours. A problem shared by many people who are overweight is that they can't express what their needs really are. Often they cannot admit that they have needs. As a consequence they rarely meet their needs. Eating foods that are sweet and fattening then becomes an antidote for the accumulation of unarticulated and unmet needs.

You can begin to address this issue by answering the questions posed by the following exercise:

IMAGINAL EXERCISE #6
MY TIME

Closing your eyes and breathing out three times, ask yourself: to whom does my time belong? See and know what you are doing with your time.

Breathe out and ask yourself: to whom does my life belong? See and know if it belongs to you.

Can you take back your time if you have given it away? Can you take back your life?

Open your eyes.

Your journal is a good place to record the answers to these questions and your understanding of what your answers mean. When questions of time recur, remember this exercise; also return to what you've written in your journal.

> *Jane's response to these questions was that she had given her time and her life to her family. When she considered whether she could take them back, she saw a policeman standing at the door of her house, forbidding her to leave. She recognized that this was how she saw her life. This was the view of things that she had constructed for herself. She was able to understand what kept her in a pattern of overeating: she had imprisoned herself.*

Chapter Four

> *As the famous Chinese saying goes, "the way out is through the door." Jane needed to determine whether she was ready to confront the challenge of exiting the familiar, comforting, and fattening frame of her everyday life. This is something we all need to contemplate. Do we have the courage to open the door and walk out into the unfamiliar and unexpected?*

Giving away all our time, filling in all the available spaces with other people's needs, feels unselfish. It is viewed that way by others, and we are proud to be thought of that way. Yet this generosity has contributed to a particular imbalance between giving and receiving. We have given away so much of our time that we have almost none left for ourselves. And what have we received in return? Rarely enough for all that we have sacrificed. Somewhere inside of ourselves we resent this situation, which seems impossible to change. We feel depleted of so much of our energy, and food seems to be the only way to replenish ourselves. We can hardly do otherwise, unless we take back some of our time.

Whatever you choose to do with your time, including giving it to others, in the final analysis your time does belong to you. It is yours to give, to whomever you choose. Can you choose to give some of it to yourself? Can you choose to diet?

Perhaps you need to repossess your time, take back ownership of your life.

IMAGINAL EXERCISE #7
FIXING THE CLOCK

Closing your eyes and breathing out three times, imagine there is a clock in front of you. Study the clock. See what kind of clock it is. Breathe out.

See that the clock is broken; it no longer keeps time.

Breathe out.

Carefully, open the clock. Slowly, one by one, take out its many little pieces. See how beautifully crafted they are. See how beautifully they work when they fit properly into one another. Dust the inside of the clock with a golden feather duster.

Breathe out.

Replace the pieces of the clock exactly where they belong. See how well the clock keeps time.

Opening your eyes, see that this is your clock. It is keeping your time, for you.

Record your experience in your journal. Draw your perfect clock.

Chapter Four

THE FEAR OF FAILING

Another excuse we give ourselves for not even getting started on a diet, which can also express an inner sense of inadequacy, is that we are going to fail. Given how difficult it is to maintain the discipline of eating a certain way, which is to say, given the difficulty of maintaining absolute consciousness in relation to an activity so omnipresent and natural as eating, dieting often seems not worth the effort. Our past failures weigh heavily on us. There is no reason to feel in the least self-confident about ourselves.

When we don't do something in the present because we have failed in the past, we bring the past into the present and allow it to determine the future. The real problem isn't the fear of failure. Holding on to the body weight we don't want is already a failure, not because there is some ideal weight human beings have to be and we have failed to attain this weight, but rather because we'd prefer not to be holding on to this weight. What is preferable about failing in the present to failing in the future is simply that present and past are already known and familiar. They are safe. They harbor no surprises.

Disappointment over past failures is difficult to overcome. Past pain is so vivid in our minds that it can overwhelm everything, including present and future possibilities. And, so, sometimes when we look into the future, all we can see is that vivid, painful, disappointing past confronting us once again.

To confront change requires courage. To confront the unknown requires faith: faith that we can handle whatever the future may bring, success or failure.

Here's an exercise that can help you face the future.

IMAGINAL EXERCISE #8
DRAWING THE CURTAIN

Breathe out three times and imagine that you are standing in front of a curtain that is made of a very heavy, opaque material. You have a sword in your hands. The sword is facing forward. All of us possess this sword. Some of us, however, have it pointed in the wrong direction.

Now with enormous force, slash the curtain in front of you with horizontal and vertical strokes. As it opens before you, see a beautiful open field, with a flower-strewn path leading forward into a luscious garden. Walk down the path and enter this garden. As you walk on the velvety grass, feel yourself similarly light and easy. Find a tree and sit down under it, leaning your back against the bark. Breathe in slowly and calmly, feeling how the tree is breathing out, giving you its oxygen, while you are giving the tree your breath. Together you form a perfect cycle. Feel yourself

Chapter Four

a part of this world of nature's perfection. Be comfortable in it. Know that this place you have found belongs to you, and you can return here anytime you desire.

Breathing out now, open your eyes.

One woman felt elated by this exercise. Suddenly she experienced her oneness with all the living organisms of the world – all the people and birds and trees and insects that were accompanying her on the journey of life.

The future can promise good things. It's important to know that. It's also important to know that you don't always have to fail in your undertakings. *You can succeed as well.*

ON YOUR WAY

So, why not set the date and get started? You are already on your way.

IMAGINAL EXERCISE #9
SETTING THE DATE

Close your eyes. Breathe out three times.

Imagine that you have a daily calendar in your hands. See that you are on the page that has today's date on it. On that page, under the date, see your present weight.

Breathe out. Now see the weight you wish to be marked to the right. Turn the pages of the calendar until you reach the date when you will weigh your desired weight.

Breathe out and see yourself as you wish to look on that date. See the clothes you are wearing. Feel and know that you are that self you wish to be.

Keeping the date in mind and with a feeling of being thinner in your body, breathe out and open your eyes. You can literalize this exercise by drawing the calendar page and your markings in your journal.

We are now ready for Rule #2.

Chapter Four

Rule #2:
You Shall Eat for No One's Reasons but Your Own

DIETING AND SELF-ACCEPTANCE

YOU are the person you are dieting for.

You shall eat for the person you are and wish to be.

You shall eat for the slimmer person who doesn't need or want any extra weight.

Rule #2 is related to Rule #1. Together they constitute the foundation of everything else that follows.

We are all so afflicted by media images of excessive thinness, that even "succeeding" in losing weight can seem like failure or, at least, too little reward for so much effort. Most of us will never be as thin as those models and actresses who form our shared public image of beauty. This is another excuse we often give ourselves for not dieting.

Dieting can seem like a no-win proposition: we diet in order to achieve what can only seem less than a success to begin with, and which we can barely hold on to even when we arrive somewhere in the vicinity of our desired slimness. Indeed, feeling too fat even when we are slim, we are likely to capitulate to the tried and true satisfaction of eating. And that is what put on those extra pounds in the first place.

Ironically, in order to eat to lose weight and maintain weight loss, we have to begin by accepting our bodies. We have to accept that we have bodies, and we have to feel that they are beautiful. We must appreciate and value them enough to want to feed them properly, which is to say, not to excess. We have to want to maximize health and a sense of well-being and loveliness. Our loveliness begins with our body and arrives at a more spiritual place only in the course of time. That's how it used to be when we were children. That's how it is now.

In other words, we must appreciate and value ourselves – including our physical selves – enough to want certain things, including certain physical satisfactions, quite literally of the flesh.

Eating to feed the slimmer self is not about self-reproach or punishment. Nor is it about expressing a grievance or a gripe against the world. Indeed, overeating may itself be an expression of just such attitudes of contempt for ourselves and others – as when, being told we haven't done our jobs well enough or that we aren't good enough mothers, we exact our revenge (against ourselves? against others?) by eating. In order to be effective, eating to feed the slimmer self has to embody our own best relationship to the world and to ourselves.

Chapter Four

Hence Imaginal Exercise #10, which expresses thankfulness and appreciation. It helps us to value ourselves properly, to consider ourselves worthy of the time and attention eating to feed the slimmer self demands. This is the exercise to do as you start to feed your slimmer self. And it should be repeated as often as it takes to remind you that you are grateful to yourself, including your body, for being who you are.

IMAGINAL EXERCISE #10
THANKFULNESS AND APPRECIATION

Close your eyes and breathe out three times.

Starting with your shoulders and your back, working your way through your body down to the tips of your toes, appreciate every muscle, organ, and gland. Tell each cell of your body that you are grateful for everything it is doing for you and everything it has done for you throughout your life. Know how every organ in your body is functioning perfectly.

Express your appreciation to every part of your body for its ability to perform. Know how your body is perfect and how your perfect body is a fit habitation for your soul.

Smile and open your eyes.

ENVISIONING SUCCESS

In chapter 3 you looked into the mirror and discovered your slimmer self (Imaginal Exercise #2). To eat for that self, you have to see it emerging. The following exercise can be done daily as you walk from one place to another. It will enable you to feel and know the thinner you that wants to be released.

IMAGINAL EXERCISE #11
THE ZIPPER

Close your eyes. Breathing out, imagine that you are standing up and see, sense, and feel that you have a zipper from the top of your neck to the bottom of your toes. Unzipping this zipper, see yourself stepping out of the excess weight that has been surrounding you. Feel the thinner you emerge into the world with a smile. Feel the lightness of your body and keeping that feeling, open your eyes.

This is a good exercise to repeat, as often as you like, each morning on arising, or while walking to the store, any time, anywhere.

> Whitney, a 21-year-old student who was studying in Israel for a year, joined one of the weight groups with

Chapter Four

many doubts. She had weighed 150 pounds since she was 18 years old, and although she was not really fat, she felt that she was just a little too pudgy to wear the more trendy, form-fitting fashions she wanted to wear. Whitney is what we used to call pleasingly plump, but she wasn't in the least pleased by it. This particular visualization, which she did faithfully each day walking to school, helped consolidate her resolve to achieve her slimmer self. It helped free her from the excess pounds padding her body, so that she could dress and feel as she wanted to. Whitney lost 15 pounds in four weeks and has maintained that weight loss for the last two years.

Another exercise, which you can also repeat daily, goes as follows:

IMAGINAL EXERCISE #12
THE PHOTO

Close your eyes and breathe out three times.

Select a photograph of yourself that you like.

See this photo on a full-length mirror in front of you. Imagine yourself lying down at the foot of the mirror with your feet touching the feet of the picture. With your eyes closed, feel the person in the photo leaving the mirror and re-covering you, from head to foot.

Open your eyes, keeping the sense of the photo within you.

One woman of 56 selected a photo of herself as a much younger woman, riding in a convertible car, with her hair blowing in the wind. During the visualization, she was able to reawaken and recover the joy of that memory. The feeling remained with her for weeks afterward.

THE POLITE "NO"

Everyone, even the people who are serving you dinner (whether they are thin or fat), have their own, often complicated relationship to food, serving it as well as consuming it. It isn't that people's intentions concerning your eating are necessarily bad. Most of us feed others (including ourselves!) out of love. But other people's relationships to food should not get in the way of what you have decided is going to be your relationship to food.

One young man who was struggling to lose weight was at a party with his wife. Another member of his weight group was also in attendance. As the man and his wife drew near to the dessert table, laden with all sorts of

Chapter Four

cakes and goodies, the wife handed her husband a dish of chocolate cake, saying, "So-and-so isn't watching: you can eat this now!"

There are other ways of showing and receiving love. Feeding a person's desire to lose weight may be a greater sign of love than forcing him or her to share the pleasure of an apple strudel or a doughnut (which is likely delicious). We have to gently educate our family and friends to this fact. We have to help them see what really counts as loving us.

There's no need to get into a hassle over this. You certainly don't have to be angry or even impolite. It is enough to admire the meal someone has prepared for you, eat moderately so as to compliment the chef, and express one's gratitude and appreciation. Likely no one is going to notice and comment on what you do or don't eat anyway, unless, of course, you talk about being on a diet. Then, everyone will probably have an opinion concerning what you are eating.

An important aspect of taking charge of what you are eating, and eating for yourself (Rule #1) is, indeed, that you do *not* tell everyone you are on a diet. The wisest course may in fact be to tell no one. One woman with 60 pounds to lose went home from her first meeting with the group and, at once, discussed her diet with her husband. Thereafter, at each and every meal, he had an opinion to express concerning what she was and was not eating. She felt completely controlled by him. Her only recourse, or so she felt, was to take back her authority by eating as she pleased, mindlessly and to excess.

After you've begun to lose weight, but still need to lose more, there will be pressure on you, applied by well-meaning friends and parents and spouses, who think you have gotten too thin or aren't eating in a balanced, healthy way. It's for you to decide what is the right weight for you. Barring actual psychological complications (like anorexia), most of us are not likely to suffer from the problem of getting too slender.

Very often, weight loss first shows in the face, where thinness is most visible. Therefore, others leap to the conclusion that we are wasting away. Most of us know where our weight lies! And, even after we have reached our desired weight, we will most probably have stores to spare.

Remember: Your diet is for you.

It is about you, and what you desire.

You decide. No one else. You and you alone.

The following exercise will help you maintain your decision to lose weight your way.

Chapter Four

IMAGINAL EXERCISE #13
SAYING NO

Breathing out three times –

   Quickly: imagine someone on the street asks you directions. See yourself not answering;

   Quickly: imagine you have just given a lecture and someone asks you a question. See yourself not answering;

   Quickly: imagine a family member, asking you for a favor. See yourself not responding.

These little exercises are not easy to do. Those of us who have been quick to respond to the requests of others have often found ourselves restoring our energies with food. We have tended to take care of other people's needs while not attending to our own. And having had the feeling that we are "giving away" so much of ourselves to others, we have felt it necessary to take something back for ourselves. We have done that in the form of sugars and starches.

This is the behavior we have to change in order to diet successfully. We can continue to say "yes" to other people's demands only so long as we acknowledge that "no" is also a possible, legitimate answer. Granting the possibility of saying "no" to others also allows us to accept other people's "no" without feeling unappreciated. Feeling unappreciated can also lead us to turn to food for comfort.

If you had difficulty saying "no" in Imaginal Exercise #13, then you were able to experience how habitual your "yes" response has become. If you can't say "no," your "yes" may have lost its true value. You are no longer choosing between alternatives. You are no longer determining and taking responsibility for your actions.

This brings us to Rule #3, which has to do with the issue of deciding, making choices, determining things for yourself. Rule #3 follows from the three questions in chapter 2: am I eating to gain weight? or to lose weight? or to maintain my weight? It turns Rule #2 inside out and tells you what you have to say to yourself when you are offering yourself food rather than receiving it from others.

Rule #3:
You Shall Never Eat Mindlessly

THE MINDFUL EATER

It's simple: You never eat without deliberately deciding and choosing what to eat.

Chapter Four

Another thing we sometimes mean when we give the excuse that we are too busy to diet is that we simply don't have the time to think about it, which – since thinking takes even less time than washing the lettuce leaf or peeling the carrot – translates into, I don't want to think about this. I don't want to think about what I put into my mouth. I don't want to think about the consequences of what I eat. I don't want to think about food, period.

Remember the three questions in chapter 2, and how much distress they caused some people.

Contrary to what some people think, most people who are overweight do not think about food all day. They do not spend their time dreaming of chocolate sodas and planning the next meal. In fact, they should be planning the next meal: the next dietetic meal. If anything, people who are overweight think about food too little. They run out of the house without breakfast. They don't feed their hunger until they are famished for food and only a bagel will do. Most overweight people just don't want to think about food at all!

Ironically, we have to do just that: we have to be conscious of what we eat, and eat intentionally, *with the intention to lose weight*.

Here's an exercise for increasing mindfulness and gaining control over your automatic responses so that you can lose weight, and later, maintain your weight loss.

IMAGINAL EXERCISE #14
MINDFULNESS

Choose some activity you do every day, like brushing your teeth, opening your mail, drinking a cup of coffee. While on the verge of performing this activity, stop for a moment: hold the toothbrush in your hand, for example, without touching your mouth; stop for one second, interrupting the motion of your hand, and then continue the brushing motion. Do this for three weeks with an activity of your own choosing, like opening the mail, closing the door, picking up a cup of coffee.

One young woman who did this mindfulness exercise using her morning cup of coffee, discovered after a few weeks that she no longer had any desire to drink coffee. Although this was not the goal of the exercise, she felt she had benefited from it nonetheless by gaining control over a particular habit, a habit she wanted to eliminate.

Whenever we want to eat something we know we shouldn't eat, we need to ask ourselves: do I really want that biscuit, bagel, banana that I am reaching for? Is it hunger I am feeling, or something else?

Chapter Four

There is a way to determine the answer to these questions.

THE HUNGER TEST

Whenever you find yourself inexplicably looking for something to eat, ask yourself: will a cucumber do the trick? a handful of cut peppers? a cherry tomato?

Not the answer to what you are looking for? If none of these foods will satisfy the feeling that you are calling hunger, then you are more than likely not really hungry.

If it does turn out to be hunger after all, real hunger for real food, then it's time to eat. Indeed, it may be a fear of getting hungry, really hungry, which is causing you to overeat in the first place (this is a reason not to let yourself get hungry; see Rule #4).

Brenda, a dieter in one of our groups, for example, objected to the rule against eating late at night (another rule we'll get to in a moment). If she didn't eat a fourth meal at night, she protested, she'd wake up hungry! And she meant it. She couldn't tolerate the notion that she might experience hunger in the morning. As a consequence she didn't eat any breakfast, an essential meal for dieters. She preferred a plate of leftovers to keep her company in bed at night to a nourishing breakfast in the morning, which she didn't have time to prepare or to eat, and which she didn't need, in any event, because she wasn't hungry! But what if she skipped that midnight snack and woke up hungry ... just in time for breakfast! A breakfast that might last her all the way to a salad and a chicken breast for lunch.

If you are feeling really hungry, then maybe what you need is a real meal. You may actually be hungry. Perhaps you didn't eat enough earlier in the day. Perhaps you gave in to the always-to-be-avoided temptation to starve yourself into submission.

Recognize what you did. Recognize that *not* eating is not the solution, and eat. But eat properly. Eat to feed the genuine, legitimate hunger of the *slender* person who needs to eat but doesn't want to tip the scales back out of balance.

Here's an exercise to help you see the consequences of automatic eating, and the alternatives that are also available to you.

IMAGINAL EXERCISE #15
THE OTHER SIDE OF THE MIRROR

Closing your eyes, and breathing out three times, imagine you are holding a hand mirror with two sides.

On the one side of the mirror you see yourself continuing the pattern of eating that has put weight on. In the mirror, see this pattern continuing on into the future. See how you look in the years to come.

Chapter Four

> Breathe out and erase this image. Now turn the mirror over. See the opposite of the image in the first mirror. See how you will look in the years to come.
>
> Find the key to your success within your grasp.
>
> Breathe out and open your eyes, bringing that wisdom and the key with you into your life.

It's OK to get hungry. And it's OK to eat. You just have to know when hunger is hunger and when it's something else. And you have to know how to feed your hunger for food and your hunger for other things.

THE SWEET TOOTH

Sometimes when you're "hungry" it's something sweet you crave. A diet candy is a good line of defense. Or a sugar-free drink.

Diet drinks do double duty, since sometimes we mistake thirst for hunger. It's useful to figure out which it is, and satisfy the real need.

When the craving for something deliciously rich and fattening beckons, you can imagine to yourself that you've already eaten the thing that now beckons you. You can taste it, feel it vanishing all too quickly from your mouth into the fatty deposits on your hips and thighs. Sometimes this quick visualization is just enough to awaken you to the fact that what you don't want and don't need is that candy bar or ice cream cone.

Here's a quick exercise that can be done any place at any time, even (especially!) at the checkout counter at the supermarket, which greets you with its enticing supply of candy bars and other sweets just when you are most exhausted from doing the weekly shopping.

IMAGINAL EXERCISE #16
THE MOMENT AFTER

Breathe out one time and, with your eyes open, imagine that you are eating the candy bar (or ice cream or whatever else is tempting you at the moment). Taste the chocolate on your tongue, swallow it, feel it in your tummy. Now imagine you have finished the candy bar. The moment of eating has passed. You feel full and satisfied.

Do you still want to eat that candy bar?

THE INNER HUNGER

Maybe when you ask yourself the question "what am I hungry for?" you will discover that the answer isn't food at all. Here's

Chapter Four

an exercise that can help you begin to unravel the feelings that are tied up inside, in what we call the non-food hunger.

IMAGINAL EXERCISE #17
THE INNER TRUTH

Closing your eyes and breathing out three times, imagine that you have access to the smartest part of your consciousness, the place where your inner truths reside. Feel yourself going to that place, and decide if you wish to know the truth. If you do wish to know your truth, ask yourself: what is the hunger that I am feeding? Name what it is you are missing in your life. See what will feed your hunger. Ask yourself: what is eating me?

Take all the time you need.

Know that food is not missing in your life. Know that food will never satisfy your hunger for what is missing.

Breathe out and open your eyes, knowing that you have learned a truth about yourself. Remember to record your answers in your journal.

CHOOSING AMONG IMPOSSIBLE CHOICES

Making choices is easier in certain circumstances than in others. And yet making a choice is almost always an option, even if it's a less perfect choice than we might, under other circumstances, choose. It's just a matter of taking the time to establish our options, set up a game plan, and slowly and deliberately release ourselves into action.

For example, you find yourself at a hotel or a business meeting where a buffet breakfast is being served. You start your day hungry, of course, as well you should (if not at breakfast, then when?), and here you are, being virtually assaulted by every manner of bread, roll, bagel, muffin, croissant, pancakes: the works!

If you fill your plate with these foods, you are going to gobble them down, a lot of them! But *if* you remind yourself that you are fully entitled to go back to the buffet any time you want to replenish your plate, *if* you fill your plate first with fruit and yogurt, white and low-fat cheese, and *if* you eat slowly and attentively, you will discover that, by the time you are ready to pile all those luscious carbohydrates on your plate, your need and desire for them will have radically diminished. The knowledge that you are eating to lose weight will guide you to feeding real hunger with real food that will not put weight on; therefore, once the real hunger is satisfied, it will hardly seem worth the effort to go back to the buffet table. Even if you did,

Chapter Four

you probably wouldn't eat more than a taste of one or another of the forbidden foods. A taste isn't a bagel. Nor is a plain bagel a bagel with cream cheese – *plus* a pancake *plus* a croissant *plus* a roll (and someone pass the butter and syrup, please).

Similarly, if you are going out to lunch or dinner, at a restaurant, whether with friends or colleagues or family, or at a friend's home, or at a party or wedding, you are going to be assaulted by lots of delicious, enticing, and (alas) fattening foods, some of which seem like rare, once-in-a-lifetime treats. *If you are hungry when you arrive at a meal or a party, you are going to eat.* And in your eagerness to eat, you might forget that you are eating to lose weight and eat anything and everything in sight.

As with the breakfast buffet, you also have control. Indeed, you have even more control. Because lunch and dinner come later in the day, you have time to prepare for them. You can eat a big salad or a vegetable soup before setting out; you can drink a few glasses of water or a diet drink before you leave the house or when you arrive; you can stuff some carrot sticks into your pocketbook and nibble till the right foods make their way onto the table.

One way or another, *never* set out for a special, festive meal ravenously hungry. In each and every group we have conducted, we have been asked the question, "but I have a wedding this weekend (or a board meeting or a birthday party); what will I eat?" as if on such occasions we suddenly lose the ability to choose for ourselves, as if suddenly we aren't the ones feeding ourselves. The answer is that we will eat what we decide is appropriate to our goal of losing weight. But we aren't going to be able to make good on that conviction if we arrive desperately hungry. It's as if somewhere in the back of our minds there is a voice saying to us (along with get dressed, fix your hair, put yourself together for the big event): save your appetite! We must ignore this command. No more saving our appetite for the main course, or dessert. We expend it instead. We use it up on the foods that will fill us up and satisfy us without putting on unwanted pounds and inches. After all, we are eating to lose weight.

The following is an exercise that can help you confront the temptations of the restaurant and avoid fattening foods on the menu. Although it is specifically geared to restaurant eating, it can easily be adapted to suit the wedding party or dinner at friends.

IMAGINAL EXERCISE #18
THE INTERNAL MENU

When you are in the restaurant, and looking at the menu, imagine (with your eyes open) that you have ordered all the foods that most appeal to you. Imagine that the food is in front of you. Taste the food. Imagine you are eating all of it. Now

Chapter Four

feel the fullness in your stomach that follows. Feel the physical discomfort. Recognize the feeling of being stuffed; your clothes feel too tight and your body feels heavy. Ask yourself: Do I want to feel that full? Do I want to fill myself with those particular foods, in those particular quantities? Do I want to leave this restaurant with a lot more fat on my body?

How do I feel surrounded with calories and fat? How does my thinner self feel?

Now order the meal.

One group member, Malka, described how she had given herself three very compelling reasons that entitled her to order blueberry pancakes on a brunch date with her husband and his family. For one thing, her husband was ordering blueberry pancakes. For another, she had been "good" for so long (even giving up going to restaurants while she dieted) that she deserved a special treat. Finally, her sister-in-law was joining them from Chicago, so this was a special occasion. She didn't want to put a damper on the good times all around.

So, what to do?

Malka imagined that she had ordered the pancakes, and eaten every last one, drenched in melted butter and maple syrup. She felt the sweetness in her mouth, and the bulky mass in her stomach. She felt overstuffed, bloated, so much fatter than she'd been when she sat down to brunch that her pants were actually tight on her. She experienced the dissatisfaction and disappointment of the eating experience itself and of her own lack of self-control.

Then she ordered scrambled eggs, no toast, thank you.

TRADE-OFFS

There are bound to be times when, wittingly or not, you will be in the presence of some forbidden food that has a more than normal claim on your desire: that once-in-a-lifetime trip to the most highly recommended restaurant in France, your child's first home-baked cake, a holiday food that comes around once a year. When those moments occur, make sure you eat what you eat only after you have determined that you indeed want to eat it. How much indulgence is necessary, you ask yourself, in order to satisfy the requirements of the experience. Are you ready to incur the consequences of indulging – because there will be consequences, of that make no mistake.

You have to say this to yourself. You have to know the truth of it.

Chapter Four

Those consequences might come in the form either of weight gain or of renewed vigilance. Indeed being strict can bring weight back into control. Newly added pounds are much easier to remove than pounds that have been with us for months and years.

Nonetheless, it is *never* a good idea to *borrow against the future*. It is an especially bad idea to indulge in the morning and imagine that we will be obedient for the rest of the day. Eating doesn't work that way. As the day wears on there is more incentive to eat, not less. And as we grow tired over the course of the day's activities, our willpower also slackens.

Also, as the day wears on, that bagel with cream cheese that seemed irresistible at 8 AM may just seem that much less appetizing or essential by dinnertime. It won't seem at all like a deprivation *not* eating it later, when some other nourishing and less problematic food is beckoning. Putting time between our desire and the food that falsely fuels it is one good way of producing the self-awareness that can enable us to say "no," without making us feel defeated and deprived.

You can test this yourself by setting a timer to go off in ten minutes. See if your desire for that particular fattening food is as intense after ten minutes have passed. It helps to eat something during the ten-minute wait, something that is compatible with losing weight.

Knowing how to postpone satisfaction is an essential element in eating to lose weight. For example, when you are on holiday, do not, during the first few days, abandon your resolve to diet. Do not eat all the luscious specialties of the place right at the start, promising yourself that you will be stricter later on. It is very difficult to do that. It's asking too much of yourself, and it will doom you to major weight gain. Rather, be strict the first several days, promising yourself to indulge later on. Then, indeed, if you require it, do let yourself taste some of the local fare.

As the days pass you will be closer to getting home, to your tried and trusted routine. There will be few occasions for error. Also, being able to postpone your indulgences by a few days will empower you. It will lessen your desire to go off your diet. Some of the foods that seemed so appetizing at the beginning of your trip will begin to seem, as you've seen them served up over and over again, less appealing later on. By the end of your trip, you may even be able to say "no" to something that, at the beginning, seemed absolutely irresistible.

Aviva, who wanted to lose 80 pounds and had already lost 50 of them, was worried about what might happen to her resolve to lose weight when she visited her family in South Africa. She had not been there in fifteen years and longed for the meats and chocolates that were her favorite childhood foods. To her surprise, the compliments that

Chapter Four

she received because of her new appearance kept her on her diet for the whole vacation. Her inner self had begun to emerge from under all the excess weight she had been carrying for years, and she felt responsible for her new image, aware that her family and friends were watching how she was eating, how she was feeding her new self. That her family and friends complimented that new self empowered her to continue to eat to lose weight during her entire vacation.

TRADING DOWN

The rule of thumb is that, in a pinch, when you are desperately hungry or simply without your own supplies of fruits and vegetables, and you find you are going to eat something that is not innocent calorie-wise, eat a lower calorie rather than a higher calorie product: bread, for example, rather than cake, or a fruit yogurt rather than a sweet.

If you are going to violate your diet, do it later in the day (or party or vacation) rather than earlier: there will be less time to compound the error. It is a known truth among dieters that if we overeat early in the day we are probably going to overeat for the rest of the day as well.

Above all: make sure that you always eat *consciously*, by *choice*. Make sure that you register the consequences and take responsibility for them. These are your decisions. Make them. Accept that you have made them. And then go on.

WHEN MINDLESSNESS IS OK

In order to eat to lose weight, you have to be mindful of what you are eating all the time. What is it about eating anyway that makes us want to be mindless about it? Why do we insist that eating has nothing to do with thinking and making choices? That somehow it would violate a law of nature if we were to begin to think about what we were eating?

The fact is that for many of us, eating is a form of relaxation. That is, we eat to relax, and relaxation seems to be an activity that, by definition, precludes having to think and choose and act.

After all, thinking and choosing and acting are what we are doing most of the day, especially in relation to family and work, and very often in relation to food. Most of us don't just dump a box of pretzels on the table and call the family to dinner. We prepare them a meal. We take time to do that, because it seems to us a legitimate and necessary expenditure of our energy and concentration. It isn't supposed to be relaxing. It's a job we do, even if it's a job we love doing. To work is by definition not to relax, which is why we go on vacation.

What happens as a result of the work versus relaxation logic is that relaxation – *our* relaxation – gets to be defined as

Chapter Four

not working. It means *not* doing for others, especially in relation to food, which is, after all, a major ingredient in our daily household lives.

Are there any other ways you might relax during the course of a day other than by eating, in particular by eating foods you haven't had to expend any energy preparing? After all, planning a vacation can take months and lots of phone calls and trips to the travel agency. Even surfing the net is a time-consuming process, as anyone who has purchased a book through Amazon knows all too well. But we don't usually refrain from ordering the book or planning the trip because it seems like work.

If you can build into your day the book or the movie or some other recreation, you might find yourself sufficiently leisured not to have to use food to relax. Or if you can come to see preparing foods for yourself as itself a form of legitimate self-indulgence – or at least an activity that is designed to enhance your pleasure in life – then you might be able to get past the false equation that an expenditure of energy fixing yourself a meal cancels out the enjoyment of eating it.

These activities, including food preparation, can, to some degree at least, substitute for the relaxation supplied by mindless eating. But only to some degree. Every day we need to eat. Therefore, every day, crowded as it is with so many activities, is going to provide at least some temptation not to have to worry about this one activity, given everything else we have to worry about. Even more importantly, eating is an activity, which unlike most other activities *is* in some very basic way mindless. It certainly doesn't take the same amount of concentration demanded by our other activities.

It's easy to see how eating mindlessly – eating to be mindless – builds on our earliest infant experiences of being fed. When we eat without thinking, when we eat whatever comes to hand, we are restored to that infant state when we didn't think about food. Food just happened to us, and we were satisfied. Preparing the meals that will best serve our desire to lose and maintain weight loss can't become mindless in this way. But it *can* become pleasurable and self-nurturing in the same way that preparing meals for our families or planning vacations can become pleasurable and self-nurturing. You deserve to focus some of your attention on yourself. You deserve to do things for yourself, because you are just as deserving as anyone else. Preparing dietetic meals can become a satisfying and even relaxing part of your daily routine. Over time, it can even become so automatic and unselfconscious as to almost count as mindlessness.

If what you are saying to yourself when you say that you don't want to think about what you eat is that you don't want to have to think about absolutely everything you do every day of your life, then you have to find ways of giving yourself other, less caloric mindless activities. Perhaps take a bath, or go for a walk. Lie down in the middle of the day, even if you don't intend

Chapter Four

to sleep, but just want to rest your eyes and cut off from the rest of the world. Ramble through a department store in a crowd when you really don't need anything in particular and you're not going to buy anything. These are all ways to be mindless in the world. And sometimes mindless is a way to be in the world, a way we need to conserve energy and reactivate desire.

IMAGINAL EXERCISE #19
THE MILKY WAY

Closing your eyes, breathe out three times and see what is all around you. Breathe out. Know that you are not a part of nature, you ARE nature. You are all of it. Breathe out. You are not a part of the world, you ARE the world. Breathe out. You are not a part of the universe, you ARE the universe. Breathe out. You are the galaxies, the stars, the Milky Way.

Everything in the world exists because YOU exist. Without YOUR vision, there is nothing. Because YOU exist, the world exists. Open your eyes.

Rule #4:
You Shall Never Eat on the Run

THE PLEASURES OF DINING

Rule #4 has to do with our more formal eating, with those three or more meals a day when we eat because eating is a part of what all of us need to do to keep healthy and alive. Though this rule has many components to it, its simple compact formulation is:

Always eat deliberately; focus on your eating; never eat on the run.

Every time you eat, know that you are eating to feed the slimmer self. Then deliberately, lovingly, enthusiastically feed that slimmer self!

IMAGINAL EXERCISE #20
THE BODY OVERHAUL

Before reading the following exercise, draw a picture of yourself as you imagine you look now. Do not concern yourself with your artistic ability. Rather, create an image of how you see yourself at this very moment. Then fold the paper in half and cut the paper into sixteen pieces. Throw the pieces of paper away, knowing that this image

Chapter Four

will now be gone forever from your consciousness.

Part I: Restructuring the Outer Body
Week #1: Before sitting down to eat, even on your way to your meal, imagine your arms and legs folding in. See your fingers fold into your hands, your hands fold into your wrists, folding into your forearms and elbows, folding into your upper arms and shoulders. See your toes fold into your feet, your feet into your ankles, folding into your knees and calves, folding into your thighs and hips. Now see all your folded limbs folding into your abdomen under your diaphragm and meeting there.

Though this exercise might take some time until you learn it, eventually it should all be done to the beat of one quick inhalation.

On exhaling, see yourself releasing your body and stretching it in all directions, making yourself taller and thinner. Now return to your normal size.

Do this exercise as quickly as it takes you to inhale and exhale, three times before each meal.

For those who cannot imagine and sense their body restructuring, see the image of your body projected in front of you on a screen, where your body contracts and tucks into itself, releasing itself as you exhale.

Part II: Instructing the Body

Week #2: Continue the first week's exercise, and add the following:

When you sit down to eat, tell yourself the content of the meal you are about to eat. Then tell your body to take in exactly what it needs and to reject what it does not need. Do this at every meal for the next two weeks.

Part III: Stretching the Body

Week #3: After completing the above two exercises, add the following:

Sit back in the chair, close your eyes, breathe in and physically bend your body over from the waist, elevating your legs and stretching them while stretching your arms out in front of you. On the exhalation see your arms and legs extending far, far out in the front of you. Relax and repeat this part of the exercise two more times.

Chapter Four

After week three stop the exercises for seven days. Repeat the cycle if you wish.

THE TRUE ENJOYMENT OF EATING

When you eat, eat. Don't read the newspaper, watch TV, talk on the telephone. Don't do any other activity that is going to distract you from what you are doing such that you lapse into absentmindedness and carelessness. Since most of us who are overweight have not really taken the time to appreciate the experience of eating, we need to pay special attention to the fact that it is enjoyable. Perhaps that is why so many religions have prayers before meals: Food is a blessing for which we can be grateful.

TASTE IS IN THE MOUTH OF THE EATER – AT LEAST BRIEFLY

It is a part of this blessing, a part of the legitimate pleasure of eating, that foods have tastes. Choose foods that taste good to you. Choose foods you like to eat.

Eat them to taste them. This means, eat them slowly. Permit the different foods their moment of truth as you chew and savor them.

Taste the different tastes of the different fruits and vegetables, meat and cheese, herbal tea and coffee.

Chew your food deliberately. Savor it with delight. As Michio Kushi advises, "Drink your solids, and chew your liquids."

And while you are chewing and savoring, put down your knife and fork. You don't need them at this very minute. At this very moment, you are tasting, not gobbling. Do not pick up your fork again until you have swallowed what you are eating, and your mouth is empty. And when you do pick up your fork again, don't overload it. You want to be able to indulge, all over again, in the experience of this taste in your mouth at this moment. People who have tried this technique discover that they begin to lose weight effortlessly, without having to force themselves to "abstain."

Eating slowly will also give your food more time to arrive in your stomach. It will stretch out the meal. You will begin to feel full *before* you have eaten every last morsel on your plate. It takes twenty minutes to feel full. Give yourself a full twenty minutes. Then decide if you want more to eat.

For the same reason, drink water, lots of it, before as well as during your meal. Water is essential for good digestion. It also fills you up. And it prepares you for the next taste.

One group member reported how she would rush through her meal so that she would still be hungry for dessert. For those

Chapter Four

of us who wish to eat to lose weight, the secret is *not* to leave room for dessert. At the end of the meal, you'll in all likelihood still have room for a taste of chocolate mousse or strawberry shortcake. But by then a taste will suffice. A taste isn't going to make you put on weight. But it will satisfy that sense of enjoyment food ought to be providing you with, which is exactly its taste!

If you're honest with yourself, how long does a taste last, anyway? Will eating the whole piece of cake be any more satisfying five minutes after having eaten it than having had just a few well-selected morsels? This is the time to remind yourself that you are eating to lose weight!

The memory of taste is in the mind, not the mouth. Five minutes after the piece of cake, five minutes after the morsel, it's going to be the same taste, the same memory.

If you should find yourself looking longingly at the chocolate cake, stop for a moment. Turn your attention to your stomach. Feel if it is full or empty. By concentrating on your stomach, you will shift the desire of your taste buds and the appetite of your eyes to the reality that you have just eaten a complete meal and aren't the least bit hungry. This shifting of the sensations has helped many of the women in our groups who have struggled with their desire to continue eating for the sake of eating and tasting long after they have "eaten enough."

YOU ARE YOUR OWN BEST GUEST

When possible put time into preparing the meal. Choose the ingredients you want to make your meal special.

Attend to aesthetic details: the plates and napkins; flowers on the table, perhaps? Do whatever will make the meal seem more satisfying and pleasurable.

Even if you can't consume your meal on the spot, but need to take it to work or eat it someplace else, you can probably manage some amount of aesthetic enhancement. Placemats are eminently portable; plastic utensils come in colors; paper plates come in designs.

And speaking of plates: use smaller plates that won't dwarf that portion of chicken or fish: it isn't really that small but a large plate can make it seem so.

Fill your plate with permissible foods, and measure out the portions of the other items you are permitted to eat (a food scale is a good piece of equipment to acquire). Eat the lower calorie foods before the higher calorie foods, so that if you do feel full, you can benefit from the maximum amount of food with the minimum number of calories.

Chapter Four

MEAL TIME IS MEAL TIME; WHEN YOU ARE TIRED, GO TO SLEEP

It is also useful to draw a boundary at the end of the day after which time you simply do not eat. Exhaustion is very often mistaken for hunger, so as we get tired we may well reach for a doughnut rather than our pillow. Late-night snacking also takes in unwanted calories when we are least in a position to burn them off, since eventually we will reach for that pillow and put our extra calories to bed with us.

You name the hour. Then brush your teeth, put on your nightclothes, and call the kitchen out of bounds till the morning.

IN PRAISE OF THE GARBAGE CAN

For many of us, leftovers constitute a particular challenge – especially if we've invested time and money in the foods we've bought or prepared. At the back of our heads is always that *waste not, want not* adage, which, in truth, speaks a wisdom we probably oughtn't to dismiss too quickly. But what if we reversed the saying and said to ourselves: *want not, waist not*.

We can reasonably ask ourselves if we are really willing to take on the consequences of eating the remainders of the kids' dinners or what our guests (in their wisdom, perhaps!) haven't seen fit to consume. Some things are more flattering in the garbage can than on our thighs. And most of us can point to the leftover cheesecake that has now become tummy and tush.

If we don't want to throw things out, we can always save them for another time or another customer. Buy small containers for those tidbits that seem too minuscule to be stored in the refrigerator or freezer, but too high in calories to be innocently consumed. Maybe you'll actually use them, when you've got a few extra calories coming to yourself or when you don't have time to buy a treat for the children. But maybe when you next look at them, they won't seem so eminently edible and attractive that you have to devour them or serve them at all.

At the very least, packing away leftovers gives you time to decide what you want to do. Time is one of our greatest allies in losing weight and maintaining weight loss. Time allows us to think. It allows us to decide.

Another trouble spot for many of us is carbohydrates – bread, potatoes, pasta, rice. Not only are these foods high in calories and therefore to be consumed in very moderate quantities, but they tend to stimulate appetite, especially in those of us who are (for whatever reasons) addicted to them.

Eating a high-carbohydrate meal early in the day can precipitate uncontrollable hunger in some of us. If you are one of those people, you might be better off not eating carbohydrates at all for a while. Or, if this seems like too much of a sacrifice,

Chapter Four

eat them later in the day – at supper, for example. Eating carbohydrates at dinnertime can minimize the consequences of the addiction, especially if you have decided that you will eat nothing after dinner.

Also, for some of us certain carbohydrates are more problematic than others. Experiment. It may well be that a morning bowl of oatmeal will satisfy you, sit heavy and cozy in the tummy, and not cause a surge in appetite later into the morning. Still, generally speaking, it is best to put off eating carbohydrates until the evening meal.

Rule #5: You Shall Never Go Hungry

THE SATISFIED DIETER

Some of us may still think that the best way to lose weight is just not to eat. Studies have demonstrated that diets of 600 calories daily are not more effective than diets of 1200 calories: twice as many calories, the same weight loss. It is also known that the longer you go without eating, by skipping a meal for instance, the more your desire for sugar products increases. Therefore, Rule #5: never let yourself get hungry. Indeed, *never skip a meal.*

The Jerusalem Diet

Likely all of us have at one time or another gone on starvation diets. Sometimes these were liquid diets, sometimes single food diets, sometimes they literally involved fasting. All of these diets were designed to take off weight fast. And very often they succeeded – up to a point. For all of them doomed us eventually to put the weight back on again just as fast as we took it off, and then some.

Part of the problem with such diets (aside from the costs to your health, which are often considerable) is that they don't change your relationship to food. Sooner or later these diets leave you feeling hungry, often quite literally! And so you want to eat, and eat a lot! And so you do.

Especially if you are used to feeling full (even if that is a feeling you may eventually be able to put aside: isn't it preferable to feel light?), feeling empty is going to be an intolerable experience. No number of promises that your stomach will shrink and no amount of scolding that you are being ridiculous about this (after all, how painful could a half-full stomach be?) is going to make that feeling of discomfort go away.

If you eat to feel full, emotionally, and if you do that by making yourself full physically, then feeling empty is going to make you feel really empty. For most of us overeaters, that is an intolerable, untenable position. And so we are going to eat, ravenously, and justifiably so.

Chapter Four

If you need that feeling of fullness (some people don't), indulge it. Just eat the foods that won't put weight on, or that may even help to take it off. In the same vein, if you need to nibble, then nibble: cut the permissible vegetables into tidbits, crumble the permitted number of dietetic rice cakes into pieces, and nosh. Chew a piece of diet gum.

There are lots of foods you can eat to satisfy your need not to feel hungry – almost every kind of vegetable, some fruits, soups, and a variety of diet products, most of which can't be eaten to excess but can be used to fill in the gaps between meals and which can satisfy your desire to nibble and feel full. Soups are an especially good diet food – nutritious, hydrating, satisfying. A soup for supper can help speed you on your way to the slimmer self. Because our diet groups have found our soups so successful and so much to their liking, we've included several of our favorite recipes at the end of this book.

Your meals should be copious – lots of salad and lots of vegetables, not just the stingy portions that used to accompany the enormous helpings of pasta and fried chicken. Eat before meals, especially if you are going out to a party or a dinner. Remember, no more saving one's appetite. Expend it instead.

If you arrive at the smorgasbord hungry, you are going to eat every fattening thing in sight. So do not arrive hungry. And if for some reason you do arrive hungry, make straight for the water or diet drinks or the permissible munchies which, more and more, good restaurants and catering halls provide. If the restaurant doesn't put carrot sticks or celery on the table, ask for them. The worst thing that can happen is that you'll pay for them in a currency far less devastating than pounds.

When attending a special event, do not eat out of a hunger for food but out of an appetite for the event or occasion. Thank your hostess, not for the size of the portion you are eating, or for the dessert you don't want, but for having invited you. A little taste of a desired food goes a long way to satisfying personal desire. A big compliment also goes far in making your host or hostess feel you appreciate their time and effort.

Similarly, when you are preparing dinner for the kids, or for your evening guests – or even for yourself! – make sure you aren't starving. The diet soda you drink before dinner, which you can still hear your mother's voice telling you *not* to drink because it will spoil your appetite, will indeed spoil your appetite! And that's the point. You don't need so much appetite, at least not for food.

If you are used to responding to that hungry feeling whenever and however you can, making potato salad for the kids on an empty stomach is going to become a nightmare. Eventually it is going to get the best of you.

For the same reason, grocery shopping when you are hungry is dangerous. Avoid it. If you are hungry when you go looking

Chapter Four

for food, you are going to buy the products that appeal to that larger, more overweight self, who is ravenous for food, food, food. If you have satisfied your hunger with a salad or an apple or a glass of water, you will better serve the interests of that thinner, more rational self, who simply doesn't need a chocolate bar to get her through the next five minutes.

If you need to feed the emptiness, feed it. Just feed it properly.

Feeding the hunger properly means using the right foods, the foods that won't put on weight. It also means determining what sort of hunger your hunger is. As you proceed in your diet, you will more and more discover that when you ask the question "is my hunger a hunger for food?" the answer will be an emphatic *no*. For now, however, as you are starting out, hunger means food, and you have to find the culinary satisfaction that will put the hunger to rest, so that you can get on with other things, including figuring out what might serve your needs better than food.

IMAGINAL EXERCISE #21
SLIMMING DOWN

While still in bed in the morning, place your hands on your stomach. Feel its size. Breathe out and imagine that you have slid two tubes easily and painlessly into each side of your stomach.

The tubes are draining off the excess fat into two small containers, the size of butter dishes. When the containers are full, you easily, effortlessly, painlessly slide them out. You take the containers somewhere where you can pour off the fat, which has left your body forever. Do this exercise for one week.

One woman with 20 pounds to lose did this exercise religiously every morning for three weeks, even though the instructions were to do the exercise for seven days. She was very pleasantly surprised one morning to feel her pelvic bones instead of a full stomach. She reported enthusiastically to the group: "It works!"

Rule #6:
You Shall Never Leave the Refrigerator Bare

PREPARING TO SUCCEED

In order to make Rule #5 feasible, we need to follow Rule #6: *Keep the right foods handy at all times.*

Do not let your cupboards go bare, and that includes filling your purse or pockets or desk. Make sure the foods you

Chapter Four

need are there and available when you need them, whenever you need them – even on the bus to work or (especially!) strolling down the supermarket aisles or while you are watching TV.

Your refrigerator should be stocked with carrot sticks and celery stalks, cherry tomatoes and red peppers, washed lettuce leaves and melon balls, and so on and so forth. Diet candies take up almost no room at all and can be stuffed almost anywhere and everywhere. What a nice surprise to put your hand in your pocket and pull out a sweet solution to the desperate feeling that you need to eat something.

Weight Watchers had a motto in the 1970s: "If you fail to plan, you plan to fail." There is a lot of truth in that. We have to take time for ourselves if we expect to lose weight, and that requires thinking ahead and buying the right foods that will satisfy our real hunger.

Smaller frequent meals spread out over the day may be more satisfying, and more calorie thrifty in the long run, than larger meals lavishly and carelessly thrown together morning, noon, and night (and late at night, again).

If you can afford to have a water cooler or perhaps an espresso machine in your place of work, do it. Or buy a lightweight thermos to accompany you throughout your day. Or put a bottle of water in the freezer the night before and take it with you wherever you are going.

Fluids are very important, especially water. They help you feel refreshed and cleansed. Water is something good you can do for your body, and your body knows that as much as you do.

When the pangs of hunger hit, for whatever reasons (psychological or physiological – which for most of us with eating tendencies comes down to the same thing), and you don't even have time for the hunger test, then it may not be the right time to figure out what to do about the hunger. You may have to feed it then and there and consult it later. So be good to yourself: put in place what you need to feed your hunger the moment it strikes without shoving surplus calories into your mouth.

If the hunger is still not satisfied, then know that it's probably emotional and not physiological. The following exercise will help you reduce anxiety and defuse tension and pain until such time as you can confront them more directly.

Remember to keep recording your experiences in your journal.

IMAGINAL EXERCISE #20
A QUIET CLEANSING

Closing your eyes, breathe out one time and imagine that you are sitting in your kitchen slowing drinking a glass of pure, clear water. Experience the freshness of the water while you drink it. See your body becoming clearer and clearer.

Chapter Four

Feel and know that all anxiety and heaviness is being washed away, leaving you refreshed, awake, and alert, full of energy and health. Breathe out and open your eyes.

You are now ready for Rule #7, which has to do with consciousness and satisfaction.

Rule #7: You Shall Never Deprive Yourself

INDULGING DESIRE

Remember: eating to lose and maintain weight is not about deprivation. It is about *choice*. It is about choosing what is best for you, choosing what you yourself want for yourself. Therefore: Rule #7 is that *you do not, under any circumstances, deprive yourself* – either in terms of eating or, more importantly, in terms of the many other pleasures in your life that are likely both healthier for you and ultimately more gratifying.

For this reason make eating a pleasurable experience, which is focused almost exclusively on the eating itself – which is to say, on yourself. Seek out the company of other dieters, in the form of weight groups or counselors, or psychologists, or even just a good friend who's willing to support you, perhaps even join you on the bandwagon.

You don't have to be a loner about this, especially if food is bound up for you in the satisfactions of social interaction and other people's affections. By the same token, protecting against old feelings of deprivation is also why, except for that good friend or group, you don't let other people get mixed up in your diet. Being reminded by your significant other or your mother that you've just violated your diet, or, the opposite, that your dieting seems to them excessive and perhaps unfriendly, is just going to force you into a corner of self-recrimination and regret.

If dieting comes to seem like a punishment rather than a pleasure, you aren't likely to stick with it. And if you did, you might have to consider what your masochism is all about. So, don't make this a punishment, and don't let anyone else make it a punishment either.

Rather than recriminating against yourself for having all this weight you have to lose, reward yourself. Take a bath, go for a walk, shop, read a good book, flip through the pages of an absolutely mindless magazine. Each of us knows what is relaxing to her, what will seem like a pleasure and an indulgence, something that is also nonfattening.

Chapter Four

THAT DEPRIVED FEELING

It's especially important not to deprive yourself, because "deprivation" is one of those words that comes up again and again as an excuse for not dieting. What does it mean that we say we "deserve" the snack foods and treats and caloric meals that we feed ourselves, which we know we don't need and, more importantly, which we have decided we don't want? Why does it feel like "deprivation" not to eat them?

When we say we deserve something, we usually mean that we've earned it, that we have it coming to us. We've worked hard and so we deserve some reward, above and beyond whatever just compensation we've received in the form of payment. We've been a good mother or wife or friend, and so we deserve to be rewarded for that, and not only with friendship and love.

Somewhere along the line, we might come to feel that doing the things we do is its own reward. Nevertheless, none of us steer that high course all the time. No matter how noble we try to be, sometimes we are going to feel that we need something to compensate us for all the time and energy we are giving out. It's the most natural feeling in the world to feel we are owed something for the things we do.

What is perplexing is why the reward for having gotten in a report on time or having run a terrific office meeting or having chauffeured the kids to their ballet lessons should be, of all things ... *a piece of cake?*

We've already given you part of the answer to this. In those earliest moments of infancy, whenever we cried, whatever it was we really wanted or needed, we got fed. And so we came to associate eating and feeling full with relief and a release of tension. Then as we grew up, this association of food with pleasure was made worse by the variety of uses to which food continued to be put, including its becoming an out-and-out reward for doing our homework or cleaning up our room and for just being a good girl. By feeding ourselves – or more precisely, *over*-feeding ourselves – some of us replicated the pattern of being fed in childhood.

Often, however, the sources of our feelings of deprivation have nothing whatsoever to do with food, even if, over time, food has come to seem the antidote to those feelings. You can trace the origins of these feelings if you wish to by reflecting on those feelings in the past.

IMAGINAL EXERCISE #33
ROLLING BACK

Closing your eyes and breathing out three times, feel within yourself your feeling of deprivation.

Now roll back ten years and see an event that, at the time, gave you a feeling of deprivation. Experience that feeling in the past.

Chapter Four

>Roll back another ten years, and another, each time seeing the event and experiencing the feeling of deprivation.
>Breathe out and open your eyes.
>Now identify those prior scenes of deprivation.

For most of the members of our weight groups who did this exercise, the scenes located crucial moments in the past when they felt they were being overlooked or under-appreciated or devalued by the many people in their lives who mattered: parents, siblings, teachers, friends, spouses.

>*One woman rolled back ten years and then another ten years, and in each of these scenes she felt the feeling of deprivation only in relation to food. But rolling back still another ten years, she came to a scene when a beloved teacher hadn't praised her for a project she felt she had done especially well, and when she went back even ten years further, she saw herself, as a little girl in a jealous spite, feeling deprived of a gift her friend had received that she had hoped to receive herself.*
>
>*Another woman rolled back to a scene when a childhood friend left her without saying goodbye. Another remembered a boyfriend she had had in her early twenties who had told her she was eating too much.*

Still another woman remembered feeling that she was inadequate and that nothing she would ever do would change that feeling. Her sense of inadequacy was the precursor to her feeling deprived.

The question to ask yourself in the present is whether you are ready to accept that feelings of deprivation from the past belong in and to the past. Can you see that the echoes of past hurts may be what you are covering over by eating to feel full? Can you dismiss these feelings as belonging to the past so that you no longer have to soothe them and sweeten them with food?

The following imaginal exercise can help you put the past behind you.

IMAGINAL EXERCISE #24
AU REVOIR TO THE PAST

Closing your eyes and breathing out three times, imagine that you are entering a forest. In front of each tree you see a person from your past who contributed to your feeling deprived or overlooked or underestimated. Meet each person head on. Tell each person, one by one, how your experience with him or her was hurtful. Speak clearly and honestly. Tell them what you needed from them and what they did not give you, what

Chapter Four

you did not receive from them. Ask them why they hurt you.

Breathe out.

Imagine that you are leaving your body and entering the body of the person in front of you. Feel what it is to be in her (or his) body, in her arms, in her legs, in her heart. Look at yourself standing there through her eyes. Feel what she is feeling looking at you. Know the answer to your question: why did she hurt you?

Breathe out and return to your own body.

Breathe out, look at the person standing directly in front of you. Understand what happened in a new way, knowing that she did not mean to hurt you. Look her in the eye, and see her disappear.

Continue walking into the forest, confronting each person from your past in the same way. See them also disappear.

Walk further into the forest until you reach an open glen. Sit down on the grass. Sense the warmth of the sun on your body. Feel the relief of being rid of past memories. Breathe out and open your eyes.

EAT THIS, DON'T EAT THIS

Though some of us might have been plied with sweets as children, most of us weren't stuffed with sweets, or with any other food for that matter. In fact, many of us who were already in a pattern of overeating as children were probably cautioned by our parents *against* eating too much! And that's another rub for many overweight people. The very same parent or grandparent or aunt or uncle who was the source of satisfaction and pleasure through food became the same person who also withheld food from us, who didn't want us to eat, at least not to excess!

To us, who were children, with a child's sense of these things, not to eat as much and as often as we wanted felt like something we deserved was being withheld from us. This feeling in relation to food is sometimes behind the sense of deprivation we experience when we see others eating foods we have acknowledged as being too fattening for us to eat.

For those of us with histories of being overweight, it may have seemed that we were given food to eat with one hand, and with the other denied it. The feeling that we deserve a reward in the form of food, and the feeling that we are being deprived when we don't get it, may be a way we have of continuing our earliest struggles with the people who once fed us.

> *As Kay described her relationship to snacking, she explained that, whenever she went into the kitchen, she*

Chapter Four

could almost hear the food calling out to her: eat me, eat me, eat me. But as soon as she gave in and ate some high-calorie snack, she immediately felt guilty and depressed. Eating between meals had been forbidden in her home. Not getting fat had been a major priority in her mother's expectations for her.

As she told her story, it was easy to see how she was caught in a vicious cycle. Snacking was forbidden to her as a child. Now, as an adult, she could permit herself that forbidden activity, without restriction and without punishment. She could rebel against an earlier prohibition. She could declare her independence. She could give herself anything and everything she wanted.

But when she ate she felt guilty. Once again she experienced her mother's reprimand. And so food became forbidden once more. And since it was forbidden, once again she had to assert her independence, defy her mother, and mother herself – with food.

Understanding her own struggle, and realizing that she now had absolute freedom to eat just as she pleased, Kay was able to break the cycle. In an exercise, she informed her mother that she was now in charge of her own eating. She would make the rules for herself.

The following exercise can help you break the chain that may still persist in your eating patterns.

IMAGINAL EXERCISE #25
BREAKING THE CYCLE

Closing your eyes and breathing out three times, imagine you see the infinity symbol in front of you. Take a golden scissors in your hands and cut the symbol so that it becomes a straight line, with a beginning and an end. Breathe out and open your eyes.

Food is one of the earliest ways children challenge their parents' authority. Learning to eat by oneself, choosing which foods one likes, and which foods one doesn't like, are all part of growing up. Sometimes this process of gaining independence is difficult, not only for the child but for the parents as well, who see it as their job to ensure the child's well-being.

> *One woman reported that after she'd lost weight her mother, who had always greeted her with a critical comment concerning her weight, looked at her speechless and then said: "I can't decide, have you lost weight or gained weight? I can't tell." For this mother, "weight" was a way she had of expressing her concern for her daughter. She didn't even really "see" it anymore, at least not in any meaningful, objective way. She literally didn't know if her daughter was fat or thin. Therefore, when the weight*

Chapter Four

wasn't there anymore, she was literally rendered speechless. She had nothing left to say.

OUR JUST DESSERTS

Don't you deserve that piece of cake or chocolate soda or plate of pasta? Of course you do: and you deserve everything that comes with that coffee and cake, as well, including being overweight.

That's the rather mean formula for a very important truth. But it's something we might say to ourselves when we are tempted by the self-deprivation excuse to eat something we really shouldn't be eating.

All of us are grown-ups. We deserve to eat what we choose and when we choose – not necessarily to reward ourselves for this or that activity, but because it is our right as adults to make these choices for ourselves. This is the sense in which we "deserve" to eat.

We no longer have to fight it out with our mothers or fathers, because we aren't children, and they can't say no to us anymore! The old battles over food are in the past. And whoever won those battles in the past, right now in the present it is only we who are fighting this battle, alone with ourselves. Is it worth keeping up the fight long after the victory – or the defeat – has been declared?

So, if you want to reward yourself with a doughnut, because you feel you deserve it, and no one has the right to deny you that, go right ahead. You do deserve it. There is no question about it.

The question, rather, is: do you also deserve what comes along with that doughnut?

Put somewhat differently, the question is: *is the doughnut worth it?*

THE PLEASURE PRINCIPLE OF WEIGHT LOSS

Even though the goal of dieting is to maintain your weight loss rather than merely to lose weight, it is important to ensure for yourself some considerable success at the beginning of your diet so that the experience of eating to lose weight can become pleasurable rather than an echo of prior deprivations or childhood struggles. Seeing the tangible results of your weight loss is one very good way of keeping on the plan. The pleasure of success in considerable measure substitutes for the misguided satisfactions of overeating.

> *Eva immediately grasped the larger goals of eating to maintain weight loss as well as to lose weight in the first place. She decided to eat as she would be eating*

Chapter Four

in the future: smaller portions, lots of vegetables, but also some variety of more problematical foods (like starches and carbohydrates), with less overall strictness in terms of maintaining the discipline. She reasoned, well enough, that if she were going to eat this way in the future, she might as well eat this way now, and get used to it. Losing weight slowly seemed the logical, rational way to go.

What Eva didn't figure on was the old economy of the psyche: if you take something away from yourself, you've got to give yourself something else in return. Eventually, your image in the mirror, drawing closer to that image you have of yourself in your head, will do just that. It will more than amply reward you by making you more of the you that you want to be. But in the meantime, while you are coming into a new self-awareness and changing all sorts of ingrained habits, the thrill of success as you watch those pounds dissolve does its own work of compensation and reward.

Failing to in any way meet her inner needs, needs that had previously been satisfied by her overeating, Eva found herself unable to sustain her diet. She quickly resumed her old eating habits and left the group — only to gain more weight than she had hoped to lose.

Rule #8:
You Shall Never Punish Yourself

SELF-FORGIVENESS

Rule #8 has to do with those inevitable moments when, with all our best intentions and determination, we swing out of control. We eat mindlessly. We eat what we know we shouldn't and perhaps don't even really want to eat. At that moment we resist the logic of inevitability: "If I've already loused this up, I might as well eat whatever I want today, or this week, or this month, or forever!" As if eating two cookies isn't worse than eating one cookie, or the whole bag worse than eating two or three.

The following exercise will help you pull yourself back into control. In fact, it's a good exercise to do when you approach a "dangerous" eating situation, like a buffet or party. You can do this exercise two or three times daily, for as long as you remember to do it.

IMAGINAL EXERCISE #26
THROUGH THE EYE OF THE NEEDLE

Closing your eyes and breathing out three times, imagine a large needle in front of you, standing on its point.

Chapter Four

> With your arms above your head, feel yourself slipping through the eye of the needle. Feel where your body snags and almost gets caught. Then feel yourself thinning out, being massaged by the sides of the needle in those places where you most need to narrow your body. Now slip through the eye of the needle.
>
> Open your eyes and sense and feel your slimmer body, which has threaded itself through the eye of a needle.

BEING GOOD TO YOURSELF

If overeating to the point of carrying around more weight than we would like has to do with a conflict between two fierce desires — the desire to eat and the desire to be thin — then it may not be enough simply to decide in favor of one of those desires over the other. Clearly, eating has provided us with some sort of meaningful satisfaction. Until the way we look can become a substitute source of that feeling of pleasure and satisfaction, we are going to be drawn back into the satisfactions of eating. And we will occasionally not be able to resist.

Reprimanding ourselves at such a moment may be just one more defense, in line with eating itself, for not confronting *why* we eat. By punishing ourselves we may worsen those feelings of lack that probably drove us to overeat in the first place. Feeling guilty for having overeaten, we will likely overeat even more, and so remain chained to the pattern of overeating.

Behaviorists tell us that we rarely have two feelings at one and the same time. When we eat, we feel full. But if the feeling of fullness is soon followed by the feeling of guilt for what we have just done – that is, eaten food that makes us fat – then, paradoxically, that feeling of guilt, rather than inspiring us to watch what we eat, drives us to eat yet again, in order to get rid of the guilty feeling. We overeat once more to bury those feelings in fullness.

This is one more cycle you can break by cutting the infinity symbol, Imaginal Exercise #25.

FORGIVE, FORGET, AND GO ON

Just as you deserve to feed the person you are and want to be, so you deserve to be generous and kind with yourself, even when you fail a little bit in your objectives. After all, overeating has hurt nobody but you.

The moment you lapse, just put yourself back on course. As in our relationships with other people, so with ourselves, we have to *forgive, forget, and go on*. Only in relation to forgiveness is forgetfulness a permissible attitude. Forget the moment before. Every moment is now, and every now is the beginning

Chapter Four

rather than the end of something. Likely you haven't even eaten as much as you fear. And even if you have, eating more isn't going to make it better, in any which way. In fact, the sooner you return to eating properly, the sooner you can correct the damage.

The moment to start eating properly is always *now*. Learning to live in the present – freeing ourselves from the past – is a part of how we have to reprogram our relationship to food.

Perhaps this is a good place to mention the bathroom scale. Scales can be useful pieces of equipment. They can give us that feedback that says we are succeeding, so that we can gain that pleasure of success that keeps us dieting. But like everything else the bathroom scale can become a conspirator against us and our objectives.

Many of us develop as problematical a relationship to our scales as to our food. If we get on the scale in the morning and it disappoints our expectations, we decide to take our revenge. We chuck the diet altogether. After all, what good has all that eating properly done? The scale hasn't budged. Likely it hasn't gone up either, but we forget that little detail. We forget that not gaining is also a form of success, since what got us to the weight we are was putting on weight, not simply staying the weight we were.

Or, if we are pleased with what the scale tells us, we might say to ourselves: aha, look at that! Stupid scale! I slipped in a candy bar yesterday and the scale didn't even notice! That's how much it matters what I eat! I'll eat some more.

Or: I'm doing so well, see even the scale says so, why shouldn't I reward myself – with food!

Some people in our group admitted that, not only had they developed a compulsion to weigh themselves, at least once if not twice daily, but that they had also developed a relationship with their scale. Hard to believe, but their scales always gave them the same message. And that was: you might as well go on eating! If they lost weight without being careful, the scale told them they had no reason to diet. And if they had gained weight when they were being careful, the scale said, it's just too hard to diet. If they had been careful and the scale told them they'd lost weight, it was time for a treat; therefore: go and eat. And if they did not lose weight even though they'd really been strict, then what was the use of dieting anyway! They might as well go eat.

Eating to lose weight and maintain weight loss isn't about the scale. It's about you and your body. The scale is doing just fine without you. It's the perfect weight for its height and build. So, put the scale away for a while. Hide it under the bed or in the closet. Put it out of sight. Weigh yourself at set intervals, preferably once a week and preferably at night, when there are no more hours in the eating day in which to compromise your resolve.

Chapter Four

Better still, weigh yourself some place other than at home, at your diet group or at a friend's or at the doctor's office. Weigh yourself where someone can remind you why the scale isn't the only determinant that matters. Also, choose a place where the setting testifies to your being in control, your being committed to what you are doing, which is controlling your weight and not entering into negotiation with your scale.

If you are eating to lose weight, and you no longer weigh yourself daily, you will begin to "receive" messages from your body and not your scale. You will feel and know that there are changes in your body that indicate that you are in control and you are losing weight. You will no longer need external confirmation of this. You will accept the truth of what you are doing. By putting the scale away, you will have taken responsibility for yourself.

Many members of our groups have found a more helpful alternative to the scale. That alternative is the simple affirmation (repeated every morning, upon rising): "I am slimmer now, and I am getting more slender every day."

Rule #9:
You Shall Exercise

TOO TIRED TO DIET

Related to the other excuses we have for not dieting is the ever popular refrain, "I'm too tired to diet."

Very likely you are very tired. Just as most of us are very busy, too busy to diet, so it is the case that most of us find ourselves too tired to diet: after all, that's what being so busy amounts to! Tiring ourselves out. Perhaps that's why we can't find time in our busy schedule to diet. We're simply too exhausted.

Once again the issue is time. The issue is who owns our time, to whom we owe our time, and how we can find time for ourselves. We have already discussed this, earlier in this chapter. Now is a good time to go back and consider to whom your time belongs.

Still, there is yet another issue involved here.

When we say we're too tired to diet, aren't we also saying that we need food in order to provide ourselves with energy? In fact, this is not far from the truth about how our bodies work. We consume calories in order that the body can convert those calories into energy. But if your body is converting your calories into fat, then your body isn't creating energy. It is telling you in

Chapter Four

the strongest possible terms that you don't need so many calories in order to produce energy.

Often, our energy needs are not quite what we think they are. By overeating and producing more body to lug around, we are actually decreasing our energy level, putting greater physical (not to mention emotional) strain on our body to do its job.

It is true that simple sugars provide a quick energy boost, and carbohydrates a somewhat more enduring one. But both very quickly fade, leaving you more tired than you were before, and also more hungry. This is one more way you get caught in the cycle of overeating.

So what do you do when you feel so tired you cannot take another step, file another report, change another messy diaper?

THE POWERS OF EXERCISE

Fortunately, a nice thing about exercise, which most people don't realize when they are feeling exhausted and quite uninterested in exercising, is that, like simple sugars and carbohydrates, it provides an adrenalin boost. Rather than fatigue us, exercise energizes us. It does what sugars and carbohydrates do, but without putting on pounds. Indeed, the opposite. It helps take pounds off and hence doubly increases your energy level.

So, when you need a pick-me-up, you might consider a simple walk around the block and even down the hall. Or a bike ride, or a swim, if you can take the time (that time, which, after all, belongs to you!). Or a few calisthenics, right there in the living room or office. You might stand up and swing each of your arms in a circle, clockwise, five times, one arm after the other, and then repeat, swinging the arms counterclockwise. This short exercise is extremely energizing.

One three-pronged plan that meets lots of needs – not only the need of energy – is: take a walk, meet someone's smile, do a small thing for someone else. It's amazing how simple actions in the here and now can raise one's spirits. And if they involve exercise, the physiological kick is similarly enormous.

But if you really can't make the time to change your clothes and head for the gym or if it's too cold outside to take a brisk walk around the block, you can do an imaginal exercise to accomplish the same goal.

IMAGINAL EXERCISE #27
THE ENERGIZING SPRINT

Closing your eyes, breathe out three times and imagine that you are going into your room and changing your clothes into your running

Chapter Four

outfit. See yourself putting on your sweats and headband. See yourself putting on your sneakers and tying the laces.

Now see yourself at the front door, leaving the house, going outside where the weather is cool and crisp, a bright sunny day, not too warm, just right for a run around the block.

Once outside feel the cool breeze brushing against you. Slowly begin to jog. Breathing slowly and evenly, increase your pace. Go full circle around the block about half a mile.

Feel and know that you are increasing your heartbeat and regulate your breathing accordingly.

See your house coming up in the distance. Reach home and enter your house. Take off your sweaty things and see yourself taking a well-deserved shower. Feel the water cascading over your body, cleansing it and freeing your spirit.

Go out of the shower and get into your fresh, clean clothes. Now, breathe out, feeling refreshed, knowing you have exercised well, burned up those excess calories and invigorated your body. Open your eyes.

WELL-BEING AND BEING WELL

Exercise is important not only to weight loss and maintenance but to good health in general. The body is a machine. It was meant to move. It was meant to do things. There is no better way of accepting our bodies than by using them as they were intended. This means putting in the right amount of energy (in the form of calories) for them to get their work done. And then letting them do their work.

We exercise the body's various parts not necessarily to become athletes, but so that our bodies don't fall into disrepair. Fortunately for those of us who want to lose weight or maintain our weight, exercising the body increases the amount of fuel we can provide them with. And this means we can eat that much more.

But exercise also helps distribute weight, and produce muscle rather than fat. It provides a sense of well-being and pride. After all, wanting to look a certain way is very much a part of a desire for just these feelings about ourselves.

That lift we used to get from a slice of bread and a cookie can now be obtained through exercise. That's something we need to remind ourselves when we are feeling depleted and tired and when only food will seem to do the trick. A brisk walk around the block, some aerobics done on the spot, and not only will we get the lift we need, but we will also burn up a few calories in the process.

Chapter Four

Tiredness is a real problem in our everyday lives, and we shouldn't ignore it. Taking care of ourselves means also getting enough rest at night, and taking those mini-breaks during the day that can help us keep pace with our schedules. But tiredness is rarely served by gobbling down a brownie or an ice cream sundae. In fact, it's probably made worse by the foods we stuff thoughtlessly into our mouths.

Most of us know that, even when we choose to forget it.

Rule #10:
You Shall Trust Yourself

THE HERO OF THE STORY

The day-to-day pragmatics of weight loss aren't going to be learned, certainly not assimilated, in a day or a week or a month – though eventually they will. Eventually, they will become as automatic and second-nature as reaching for the first tidbit to come to hand, with the one difference that these new habits already include a place for self-reflection and consciousness.

Until they are automatic, however, we have to be in conversation with ourselves. We have to talk to ourselves, as often and as loud and in whatever language (words, images) we desire.

We have to remind ourselves what the rules are. We remind ourselves why we want to follow these rules. And, finally, we remind ourselves that we are capable of reminding ourselves, that we are creatures of consciousness who decide what we will or will not put in our mouths, and that we can be *trusted* with making these decisions for ourselves.

Trusting yourself is also the best way of maintaining your new relationship to food. No matter how much you psych yourself up for this, no matter how willing you are to believe what others (including us) tell you about weight loss, in the final analysis you are going to have to make this diet work for *you*!

This means that you are going to have to adapt this diet for yourself, for your own individual needs and preferences. And you are also going to have to let it change over time, as you enter into a new relationship to food and begin to eat in new ways.

No one is going to be able to solve all your problems for you except you. No one is going to be able to answer all your questions for you except you.

So you are going to have to listen to yourself: listen even to your complaints and excuses, in order to understand what they mean, what it is that you are really telling yourself about yourself and your eating. And then you are going to have to find ways of responding to those needs and desires that you yourself are expressing. Finally, you are going to have to trust yourself

Chapter Four

to be honest enough and smart enough about yourself to find the solutions that work for you, solutions that will enable you to be who *you* choose to be.

In his book *Healing Visualizations*, Dr. Gerald Epstein suggests that if you are down on yourself, it is probably because you are comparing yourself to someone else. You need to recognize that you are incomparable, that there is no one like you in the entire world.

The following exercise from Dr. Epstein's book is designed to bolster self-esteem and self-confidence. It can be done twice a day for one or two minutes, for twenty-one days. It goes like this:

IMAGINAL EXERCISE #28
BE YOUR OWN HERO

Close your eyes. Breathe out three times. Become your own hero and master. Acting as your own hero, see yourself overcoming the obstacles in your life, one at a time. See the obstacles dissolving into smoke and disappearing. Breathe out and open your eyes.

You can now go on to chapter 5, which is about eating to maintain the weight loss you have succeeded in making happen for yourself. If you prefer to wait until you have reached your ideal weight or until you feel you have assimilated the material thus far, please do so. Another important, if largely unspoken, rule about eating to lose weight and to maintain your weight loss is that you have time – all the time you need to realize your goals. Take your time. You have your whole future ahead of you.

Chapter Five:

Stepping into the Future;
Maintaining Your Weight Loss

"Energy is the essence of life. Every day you decide how you're going to use it by knowing what you want and what it takes to reach that goal, and by maintaining focus."
—Oprah Winfrey

This chapter is about maintaining your weight loss. If you have not yet reached your desired weight, you might want to put off reading this chapter for a few weeks, or until you achieve your target weight. If you have achieved your desired weight, then:
CONGRATULATIONS!
Read on.

EATING FOR THE FOREVER ME

As you now know, eating to lose weight can be done! It is not necessarily a simple proposition. It is, however, eminently doable. Likely there were even moments along the way (especially as the weight was coming off) when dieting became a source of satisfaction and pleasure in and of itself. At times, it was probably more satisfying than eating per se.

Maintaining weight loss is just as doable as losing weight, though it does provide challenges (as well as satisfactions!) uniquely its own. Essentially, maintaining your weight loss is nothing more and nothing less than a continuation of the project of losing weight – on even easier terms. Its major rule is: **do NOT resume your old relationship to food – either in terms of *what* you eat or *why* you eat.** Here, as before, *mindful eating* and *making choices* are the key concepts.

MINDFUL EATING AS A WAY OF LIFE

The miracle diet, as we said in chapter 4, is the diet that *you* discover is the best for *you*. Remember Rule #10: *Trust yourself*. You know yourself better than anyone else does. You are the one who has been eating to lose weight. It is you who has learned which foods put weight on and which foods help take it off. You've also discovered which foods you like and which you don't like. *You've discovered your own miracle diet!* Eating to feed the slimmer self means eating the healthy, nonfattening, and satisfying foods that you've discovered nourish your healthier, trimmer body.

Of course, now that you've reached your desired weight, you can, on occasion, eat some of those foods you avoided when

Chapter Five

you were eating to lose weight. And you can eat more than you ate when you were eating to lose weight. Your body is that same marvelous machine that takes in calories in the form of food and puts them out in the form of energy. If you don't eat more than your body needs to do its daily work, you will *not* gain weight. It is as simple as that.

This means, however, that if you resume eating in such a way that you are taking in more calories than your body can burn off as energy, you will regain the weight you've lost. Therefore, while you can relax your diet a bit once you have reached your desired weight, you still need to remain *mindful* of what you are eating. You need to continue to make *choices* about what you eat and when and how much.

At least for the moment, repeat to yourself the questions from chapter 2:

1. Am I eating to gain weight?
2. Am I eating to maintain my present weight?
3. Am I eating to lose weight?

Make sure that what you are eating corresponds to your objective, which is now to eat to maintain your present weight.

There are several ways to do this. You can make sure that every one of your meals, every single day, is designed to help you maintain your weight. Or you can arrive at your perfect balance by counteracting meals of less slenderizing foods with meals eaten "to lose weight." You may, for example, eat to lose weight for five days of the week, and then loosen up for the remaining two days. You've still got to avoid stuffing yourself or eating to excess. You've still got to prefer lower-calorie to higher-calorie foods. *Mindfulness* is the watchword. *Mindful eating. Mindful choices.* But you can now begin to balance those days of greater strictness with less strict observance (when you do indulge in that bagel or sweet or an extra helping of meat).

Because you are eating to maintain your weight loss, it is more important than ever *not* to resume or suddenly develop a self-defeating relationship to your scale. Our weight fluctuates from day to day, and is different at different times during the day. If you cannot tell your weight by how comfortable you feel in your clothes, then you will need to weigh yourself. But do not do that more than once a week. When the scale indicates a weight gain of 5 pounds, which can happen even if we are doing our best to remain conscious of our eating, it is time to have soup for supper for a few days. Weight that has recently come on will come off again just as quickly.

In the preceding chapters we gave you ways of making the venture of losing weight simpler. These included some simple, fairly straightforward rules and techniques for managing your eating. They also included guided visualizations that both helped you to locate your reasons for overeating and also enabled you to see your transformed self. Visualizing the future

Chapter Five

self helped that self come into being. What you need to do now is to keep in mind that it is that self – this new self! – you are now eating to feed.

For some of you, it is enough to know this. You've changed your habits. You've learned conscious eating. You've made your choice. You will maintain your weight loss by keeping your slimmer self in mind and eating to feed her. You will remain conscious of what you are eating. And you will eat consciously to maintain your weight loss. You have arrived! Trust your wisdom.

The following exercise will help you on your way as the thinner, sleeker person you have become.

IMAGINAL EXERCISE #29
KNOWING WHAT YOU NEED

Closing your eyes and breathing out three times, see yourself walking on the pathway leading into your future. Stop to rest, walking off the road into a small glen, surrounded by trees.

Breathe out.

Feel the coolness of the air.

See a wise woman enter the glen and sit down beside you. Ask her to share her wisdom with you. Ask her if she can give you something to take with you into your future, something to

> help you remember what is most important to
> you on your journey.
> Receive her wisdom as a gift. Thank her,
> and get up and leave the glen.
> Returning to your road, breathe out and
> open your eyes.

For those of you who feel less certain concerning your ability to maintain your weight loss, or for those of you who have failed to maintain your weight loss in the past, do the above exercise and then read on. You, too, will be able to maintain your weight loss. That is what this diet plan is all about. It just might take a bit more effort not to lapse back into old eating habits and to remain conscious of what and why you eat.

For some people maintaining their weight loss is actually more difficult than losing weight. With the thrill of watching the pounds come off now over, and with the prospect of a lifetime without this thing called casual snacking or gourmet eating or whatever we call our patterns of eating too much – which did, after all, satisfy lots of our needs (even if it created problems as well) – some people feel simply that they can't continue to eat this way, at least not forever.

Now, even more than before, you have to have some clear picture of how you want to look. And you have to have ways of preserving that slimmer self. Many of the techniques and visualizations in the preceding chapter are pertinent here as

Chapter Five

well. There is no shelf life to imaging. The exercises are good for as long as they are useful to you – for the rest of your life. That's why keeping a journal was important, and why you should continue to keep one now, to record your responses to the old exercises you now revisit, and the new ones you will learn to help maintain your weight loss.

Remember: *you* were the one who wanted to be slimmer. Nor was that desire for slimness a desire for one short instant of feeling slender. It expressed a wish you had about the way you would look from now on. So, if you find yourself, having lost the weight you wanted to lose, suddenly doing precisely what your decision to go on a diet told you not to do, then you might try the following exercise.

IMAGINAL EXERCISE #30
KNOWING THE TRUTH

Closing your eyes and breathing out three times, see yourself sitting alone on an empty beach on a warm, sunny day. Feel the cool breeze coming from the water, hear the waves lapping the shore. Gazing out at the horizon, ask yourself the following questions:

How do I feel now that I am slender?
Do I want to regain the weight I have lost?
What must I do to remain as I am now?

Hear the answers to your questions coming to you. Remind yourself to appreciate your body and be grateful. Smile and open your eyes.

Trust the answers that you receive. They are the truth for you now, as logical or illogical as they may seem.

WHAT DIFFERENCE DID IT MAKE? KICKING THE EATING HABIT ONE MORE TIME

Does being slender change your life? No, not really. What it changes is your body. Even if you were to achieve what you imagine is the "perfect" body (as presented to us by popular culture), you would still remain with all the same old issues of your life – though, of course, now you would be slimmer, which isn't anything to sniff at! Your issues, though, are what set you on the course to overeating in the first place. And now that you are thin, you confront the same issues all over again. That is the personal food chain in a nutshell.

Losing weight kept you, like most of us, in the game. Now that the challenge has been met and the weight is off, you may find yourself without that rush of pleasure that accompanies weight loss. You may feel disappointed, even depressed. Your life hasn't changed all that much, even if your dress size has. You are still who you were, still in the same place with the same old

Chapter Five

issues. Your same sadness and worry continue to inhabit you. Indeed, you may feel more despondent than you felt before you lost weight, since now eating, which once sustained you, is no longer a source of comfort.

This is the danger point for most of us. Once again we feel ourselves craving something. We wonder how we can now sweeten our sadness, fill our emptiness. For many of us losing weight has exposed what our eating had so long covered over. Naked and vulnerable we may look to clothe ourselves once again.

Now is the time to remember that eating to cover over feelings does not make those feelings go away. It only covers them over. It only makes us fatter. Sometimes it is enough to know this to keep yourself conscious and eating mindfully. Sometimes it is enough to remind yourself that, at least now, whatever your worries and cares, you are at least thinner and feeling better physically! That isn't an insignificant difference in your life, even if it isn't all the difference in the world.

Still, our relationship to food goes all the way back to before we can remember. It is a habitual part of our behavior, especially in relation to the psychological or emotional jobs eating does for us. Sometimes, feeling slimmer isn't quite sufficient to keep us from the satisfactions eating has provided. We have to keep up the effort of breaking old habits by keeping ourselves mindful of the difference between eating to nourish our bodies and eating to cover over our frustrations and disappointments.

Not resuming our old relationship to food means *not* returning to food to satisfy all those old psychological reasons that once led us to overeat. We were able to overcome those reasons while we were dieting. Now we must guard against their return. This is the greatest challenge of maintaining our weight loss: keeping at bay all those emotional jobs food used to do for us.

The following exercises will help you get rid of the mindless recourse to food as a way of anesthetizing yourself against sad or uncomfortable feelings.

IMAGINAL EXERCISE #31

MAGNIFYING AND ERASING THE HABIT

Close your eyes and breathe out one time. Select an eating-feeling you wish to be rid of, like eating when you are angry, lonely, bored, or disappointed – whatever emotion you believe leads you to the refrigerator.

Recall the moments when this habit was in full force.

With a magnifying glass in your hands, examine this habitual behavior from every angle. Then wipe it away to the left. Breathe out and open your eyes.

Chapter Five

The following exercise moves in the same direction. It can help you see your past behavior, your present transformed behavior, and your behavior as you would like it to be in the future.

IMAGINAL EXERCISE #32
THREE DOORS

Closing your eyes and breathing out three times, see yourself standing in front of three doors.

Open the door on the left, the door to your past. Enter the space and see the habit you developed there, which you need to understand as a part of your past. Accept the understanding you receive there. Leaving the space, close the door behind you.

Breathe out.

Open the door in the middle, the door of the present. Enter, taking your understanding of the past with you. See what is there, what habits you are still expressing in the present that you need to understand. Accept the understanding you receive there. Leave this space and close the door behind you.

Breathe out.

Open the door to the right, the door to your future. Enter the space, taking with you the understanding that you received from your past and your present. See what is in your future that you wish to achieve, without your old habits. See what you need to understand. Accept what you receive there.

Breathe out one time and open your eyes.

MORE ON REASON, REASONS, AND WHY WE EAT

What if simply knowing that your reasons for eating are emotional rather than physiological isn't enough to break unconscious and habitual overeating?

We all know that the "reasons" we have for doing certain things in our lives don't always derive from that rational, cognitive part of our mind we call *reason*. Yet we call them reasons, as if everything we do in our lives is logical, reasonable, even natural. One of the purposes of guided imagery has been to dislodge our thinking from the ordinary, everyday pathways of logic and reason. Not because logic and reason are bad things. Quite the opposite. Much of this book has been about making deliberate choices: the best, most meaningful, rational *and* reasonable choices we can make concerning our bodies and our lives. It has also been about taking responsibility for those choices. It doesn't get more rational than this.

Chapter Five

But for those of us who overeat, the ordinary pathways of logic and reason were making us behave in ways that made it impossible for us to achieve something we wanted: namely, slimmer bodies. Logic and reason said to us, you are hungry, you have to eat, and so we ate. It was as simple as that. And so in order not to eat every time eating seemed the reasonable response to what we were feeling, we had to circumvent these messages. Indeed, we had to circumvent those pictures of ourselves that told us that we could never be other than what we were: overweight. That was what visualizing did for us: it helped us to circumvent the doubts we had about whether we could succeed in losing weight. It helped us navigate around the apparently normal, natural feeling that when you feel hungry, it's time to eat. Maybe, we learned, in the internal world where all things are possible and imaginable, feeling hungry isn't about food. Maybe, we discovered in that world, we can do and be everything we wish to be. Why not?

One woman in our group came to question why it was that she would overeat to the point of pain. She suddenly recognized that the pain that came from feeling stuffed smothered other feelings that were even more painful and that she could not tolerate – including the feeling of being empty. But the feeling of being empty, she gradually began to realize, offered an opportunity: the opportunity of entertaining some new truth. To make space for the truth, she learned, your body has to be empty of the past. Sometimes it is easier for us to feel stuffed rather than face the truth that is confronting us, precisely because the truth means the death of the past. For us overeaters, the death of the past means no more excuses for overeating.

It is not unreasonable to like food. It is not unreasonable to want to eat. It is not even unreasonable to eat in order to cope with the tensions and frustrations and dissatisfactions of our everyday lives so that we can function better. Lots of people eat for such reasons. Some of these people don't gain excessive weight. Of those who do, there are those who don't care that they are carrying around extra pounds. All of us have the right to make these determinations for ourselves. And all of us more or less know when we are happy. We know when we have achieved a balance that is good for us. But having gone on a diet, having eaten in order to lose weight, you *do* care about your weight. Maintaining your weight loss is the next step in that process that *you* have decided for yourself.

The only issue, then, is *how* to implement what you want for yourself. If you discover that you are eating in order to feed anxiety and sadness, and if you discover, further, that eating in this way is putting on weight that *adds* to those feelings of depression and despair rather than relieving them, then you have a responsibility to listen to what your behavior is telling you about yourself and act on it.

Chapter Five

The question is how one "listens" to behavior, and, more to the point, how one changes it. Determination, reason, willpower, and making choices are our important tools for changing our relationship to eating. Still, as we all know, eating habits are among the most difficult habits to change. Therefore, a little basic psychology is in order, to strengthen those skills of mindful decision-making – *mindful eating* – that we have already put in place.

BECOMING EVEN MORE MINDFUL

We all try to protect ourselves against whatever in life makes us anxious or uncomfortable by developing behaviors (most of them quite automatic and unconscious) that ward off emotional danger. We have done this since we were children. And we will continue to do so, no matter how self-conscious and self-aware we become. Without such defenses we would feel too unprotected and vulnerable. Defenses defend us. And we need them.

Sometimes, however, our defenses and habitual responses outlive their usefulness. They no longer work as well as they once did. Or they interfere with our getting something else we desire. They keep us defended in a way that protects us from threat or danger but only by exposing us to some other threat or danger. All our defenses are unconscious mechanisms that "kick in" when we feel emotionally vulnerable.

Everyone's story is different. Everyone's enactments in the world are produced by his or her subjective experience of that world, both in the present and in the past. Therefore what we have to say to ourselves, when we are confronted with behavior we want to understand, is this: if I react this way in this particular situation, it is because of who I am. After all, we remind ourselves, other people react differently. They react for their reasons.

It is often easier to see through other people's defenses than our own. This is because their reasons for doing things in a certain way (their defenses) are designed to protect them from what they, and not we, find emotionally challenging. We don't need to protect ourselves from these things in this particular way. Our own reasons are less transparent to us, as when we find ourselves overeating and gaining weight.

Many of the successful dieters in our groups were eventually able to see that overeating had served, initially, as a successful defense. It protected them when they felt they needed emotional protection. What they also came to see, however, is how this defensive strategy, which had once been useful and effective, had now become dysfunctional. It caused them to gain excessive weight. The question they all had to address was whether they could employ their newly acquired mindful knowledge of their behavior in order to block defensive eating, to lose weight and then to maintain their weight loss.

Chapter Five

The following exercise can help you achieve the clarity of internal vision necessary to bring into conscious awareness the unconscious motives behind your eating.

IMAGINAL EXERCISE #33
THROUGH A VEILED WINDOW

Closing your eyes and breathing out three times, imagine that you are in a darkened room. The window before you is heavily curtained, the blinds drawn, and the window panes dirty and shut tight. Approach the window, and slowly open the curtains. See the first shafts of light coming through the drawn blinds. See what you can see through the slats of the blinds.

Breathe out and slowly raise the blinds. See what you can through the dirty windowpanes. Wash the windows quickly, with a sponge and water, and now look through the window again. Open the window, feel the cool, fresh breeze on your cheeks, gaze out far into the distant, unobstructed view. See what is outside the window that you were unable to see before. See into the distance with new clarity.

Breathe out and open your eyes.

TALKING TO YOURSELF

None of us is likely to ever become completely transparent, even to ourselves. However, sometimes, especially when we find ourselves confronted by contradictions in our behavior, or when we find ourselves responding and reacting in ways that no longer seem to us appropriate and useful, it becomes possible for us to glimpse – if ever so partially and briefly – the reasons for our habits. Then, perhaps, we can get into the tiny space between our feelings and our actions and change those actions. We can get ourselves off automatic pilot, and consciously determine what we are going to do in a given situation.

Many of the guided visualizations in this book have done precisely this work of revealing to our external rational minds something of our more emotional, reactive inner self. The visualizations have shown us in a direct and immediate way *why* we do certain things and *where* certain patterns in our behavior originated. They have enabled us to see how we might behave differently, and what the consequences of such changes in our behavior might bring. Because a visualization is a picture that emerges from the less conscious, less guarded part of our selves (the imagination, the heart), it bypasses most of our defensive structure. When we are imaging, we do not need to defend or protect ourselves as we do in our day-to-day lives. We are able to reach inside and discover our past, before we developed cover stories to conceal what happened there. We can see the present

Chapter Five

and imagine the future. When we visualized our future selves, we saw past our defenses. We put our reasons and justifications and rationalizations behind us.

We can also do that through talking to ourselves and listening to what we say. Even though words are a part of the rational apparatus that often serves to keep us stuck in bad behaviors, words also contain our pictures of ourselves. They, too, can provide us with answers *if* we are willing to take them seriously, *if* we are willing to ask ourselves the question: what do I really mean when I say, for example, that I can't maintain my weight loss because eating to lose weight or to maintain my weight loss is too boring or punishing or unhealthy? What is it that we are saying about ourselves, and our relationship to eating, when we make those statements, especially when we know they are going to keep us doing something we don't want to do: namely, remain overweight?

SO WHAT'S YOUR EXCUSE NOW?

We've met some of the excuses for not dieting in chapter 1. What are some of our excuses for resuming our old eating habits, and how might we outwit or outmaneuver our own defensive strategies?

Chief among the excuses for not continuing to eat in such a way as to maintain weight loss is that diet foods are B O R I N G. What do we mean when we say that?

IN DEFENSE OF THE LOVELY LETTUCE LEAF

It doesn't hurt to remember that for some people lettuce leaves – and carrots and green peppers and melons and peaches – are not boring in the least. Just watch a young child discovering the world of food for the first time. All the foods are equally fascinating, each of them equally worthy of time and attention and taste. Most of the time a slice of bread can't hold a candle to that cherry tomato brimming with juice and color and shine. Watch what the young child grabs for, and remember: not everyone prefers potatoes, rice, and bread.

Nonetheless, for some of us diet foods do seem boring. Is there anything we can do about that?

IMAGINAL EXERCISE #34
BOREDOM AND ITS DISCONTENTS

Close your eyes and breathe out one time. See a plate of "boring food" in front of you. See what is on that plate. Breathe out. Now see in front of you a plate of food that is not boring. See what is on that plate.

Breathe out and open your eyes.

Now ask yourself the question: what is food to you, when it isn't boring? What word would you use to describe that food? "Interesting," perhaps?

Chapter Five

IN THE INTERESTS OF EATING

But "interesting" just doesn't seem the right word for food, does it? After all, there isn't anything more intrinsically interesting about a potato or a slice of bread than a lettuce leaf or a cherry tomato. If carbohydrates and sweets seem somehow more "interesting," then we must mean something very specific by the word *interesting*.

Perhaps it is our lives that lack interest, not what is on our plates. Perhaps we eat out of boredom.

Foods may provide interest and make our lives interesting because of their associations with our past. Foods that were fed to us by our parents and friends bring with them mental associations.

One woman stated that the remedy for all her childhood illnesses was tea and lemon. This drink was thereafter associated in her mind with the loving attention she received when she was a child. Fortunately for her, tea with lemon isn't fattening. Others in the group were less fortunate, however. For them the loving treats consisted of cake and cookies and ice cream, rice and beans and fresh bread. The poor lettuce leaf doesn't stand a chance against such childhood memories.

THE LOVE OF EATING

Certain foods, then, are a way we have of drawing close to experiences of love and nurture in the past. It is useful to recall that and to separate out the feelings from the food.

Sociability – and love and warmth and nurture – are things we crave. And very often, these are things that, in our culture at least, take place around a dinner table or a cocktail table or the buffet line. Hence, we associate joyfulness with food, and we tend to overeat when we are with other people. If you can recognize that being with other people is the source of your happiness, and not the food, you can check that tendency to overeat around the dinner table.

You can also seek out the company of others, as a substitute for eating or as an accompaniment to eating properly. Being with other people you care about and who care about you is a goal unto itself. It doesn't necessarily require eating at all! It certainly doesn't require eating to excess. If you find yourself among family and friends, focused on the dinner rolls or the dish of cashews, you might just move them away from you and remember: friendship is about people, not dessert.

One of the reasons diet groups work is that they provide a framework of other people who care about what is happening to us, and care about it in one of the key contexts that have come to matter to us: food. Diet groups also provide accountability: we become responsible to someone else's expectations that we will stick to this food plan and that we will lose weight. And this is also related to involving others where others have always been involved: in our eating.

Chapter Five

Just as in the past we let others take responsibility for what we ate, so now, in the present, we surrender some of our self-control. This surrender was an important part of our dieting, and it continues to be important as we eat to maintain our new, healthier weight. Many of us express our autonomy and independence and sometimes even our defiance by eating foods we all know only add weight to our bodies. Dieting means that we can permit ourselves to "let down our guard" and experience someone else's concern for us, which is, after all, part of what love is.

ACCEPTING LOVE, GETTING HELP

In the final analysis, we are all responsible for ourselves: that's why consciousness-raising is a major part of the process of changing our relationship to food. Adults make choices, and we are adults. Nonetheless, there is nothing wrong with needing and taking help. That armor of fat we have constructed over the years between ourselves and the world is concrete evidence of our total self-sufficiency. We no longer need it.

Part of the irony of our relationship to food is that, just as it was an expression of love, so it was also a place of contest. By feeding ourselves we became independent of our caregivers, and often punished them in the process. Finally, it was a way we had of doing without them. We learned to feed ourselves.

Letting other people back into our lives might be a far better way we have of retrieving past love than keeping people away. Making space for other people in our lives paradoxically helps fill the empty spaces food covers over. We trade one set of spaces for another and acquire breathing room, space to move in. It's certainly worth a try.

LETTING YOURSELF GO – IN CALORIC MODERATION

In the early stages of any diet, as in any change of habit, we tend to stick very closely to a set routine. This is in fact an important part of the process of changing our relationship to food, as we have seen. Against the background of the kind of mindless eating we were doing, which is to say, against the background of having made all the wrong choices concerning our eating in the past, we needed, for a period of time, the discipline of *not* making any choices at all. We needed to let others, the experts, the new mothers who were going to mother us in a more calorie-efficient way, make these choices for us.

That is why so many diets feature a set menu, or limit you to a single food, or a single kind of food. On Monday you eat all the grapefruits you want. On Tuesday, you eat all the chicken. These diets work in part because your calorie level drops: after all, how many grapefruits or chicken breasts are you going to eat

Chapter Five

on a given day? But they also work because there is no temptation or room for compromise. You can't make a mistake because there is no room for error.

Eating to maintain your weight loss can indeed become boring if you are afraid to try your wings and become a bit more adventurous concerning what and how you eat.

> *Stanley, a 50-year-old member of the group, weighed 202 pounds in April and successfully lost 32 pounds in six months. He attributed his success to his absolute diligence in not eating his wife's freshly baked breads. What will happen, he worried, if I eat a slice of bread? Will I immediately bounce back to my former weight? Will I gradually lose control and start overeating again? Stanley couldn't trust himself to eat one slice of bread and still maintain his dieting discipline. He was afraid to eat anything that wasn't already a part of his diet.*
>
> *Because he was afraid of failing, Stanley denied himself the genuine possibility of varying his diet and making choices – good choices that would enable him to maintain his weight loss. Dieting became boring, and boredom is one classical excuse people give themselves for overeating. Stanley was in danger of getting caught up in a bad cycle all over again. Coming to see this, however, and confront it, Stanley was, over time, able to trust his ability to vary his menu and still maintain his weight*

loss. Eighteen months later, Stanley has remained trim and healthy and continues to enjoy an occasional slice of his wife's baked bread.

For some of us, making choices was exactly what we were fleeing from the start, when we ate whatever came to hand, without calculating the consequences and without taking responsibility for ourselves. By not making the choice to occasionally eat that slice of bread, our gentleman dieter was running the decided risk of setting himself – through the route of boredom – back onto the path of overeating.

IMAGINAL EXERCISE #25
VANISHING THE FEAR OF OVEREATING

Close your eyes. See yourself breathing out your fear in the form of billowy gray smoke. Continue exhaling your fear into a huge balloon in front of you.

When the balloon is full, tie it, and with one strong breath, blow it into the sky. See it become a distant star.

Breathe out and open your eyes.

Behind the boredom excuse – like so many of our excuses – is the underlying excuse of them all: the fear that we might fail. Just as the excuse of boredom may turn out to be a cover for

Chapter Five

discovering what is genuinely "interesting" in one's life (or what isn't), so the fear of failure, it turns out, may be primarily a fear of success. Perhaps that's why, when we've succeeded in losing the weight we want to lose, we immediately allow ourselves to gain it back. We are afraid of confronting the opportunities that being thinner has made available to us.

TIME TO CONFRONT THE FUTURE

One reason some of us eat is to fill up the empty hours of the day. Eating, after all, is an activity. It is a form of doing something. Sometimes, taking time to nibble something is just a way of justifying taking time off from something else we are doing and don't want to be doing.

For many of us, it is simply very hard not to be doing anything at all. We can't just sit in a chair and stare into empty space. We call that being bored, and we fill in the space of our boredom with eating, because that, at least, does seem like *doing* something.

Of course, as we have already seen, eating is *also* a way of not doing anything. It is a way of being mindless. So in a sense eating to appease our boredom will in the end only increase our feeling of being bored and lead us to eat some more. If we can come to see that eating adds absolutely nothing to the not-doing of sitting in a chair and staring into space, then perhaps we can permit ourselves the exquisite luxury of literally doing *nothing at all*: just sitting in the chair and staring into space.

Sometimes it's OK to do nothing.

Sometimes nothing is just the right thing to be doing. It is when we experience nothing that we permit something else – something new and unforeseen – to happen.

TAKING CHANCES

Sometimes it's this new and unforeseen option that we are warding against, when we keep ourselves stuck in the past. Boredom is sometimes a name we give to the experience of the "moment before": the moment that precedes the next moment, when something is about to happen. For many of us, being in that moment before, with the future open and uncertain before us, is frightening. We don't know what the future will bring. And so we rush in to supply ourselves with a "future" that is simple and familiar and safe: we eat.

Because we find it difficult to imagine or discover what the next moment might bring, because we find it hard to allow the future simply to unfold, we avoid anticipation and uncertainty by eating. But when we do this, when we substitute something which is safe and familiar for something that is unknown, then what we are really doing is returning to the past. The past does not inspire fear. It keeps us safe. It also keeps us unhappy.

Chapter Five

If you experience your life as not being exciting or fun, then you might have to risk asking the question: how can I make my life more interesting? It might be something small – such as finding a new hairstyle or social club. It could be more substantial, like finding a satisfying job. And sometimes it's even larger than that.

IMAGINAL EXERCISE #36
A QUESTION OF INTEREST

Closing your eyes and breathing out three times, see a golden pen in your hand. Raise your hand and write the following question in the sky: What do I need to do to make my life more interesting?

See the letters dissolving into the sky, forming a big cloud.

Breathe out.

Watch the cloud suddenly break open. Sense the answer to your question coming to you from the sky.

Open your eyes.

When we ask the question "where is the failure of interest in my life that I should use something so basically uninteresting as an ice cream pop or cherry tart to supply it?" it is possible that we will discover that the causes of our discontent are things we can do nothing about. Maybe that is part of the reason we didn't want to ask this question in the first place. Being overweight kept us from confronting the sad truth that sometimes we don't have solutions for all our problems. The painful loss of a loved one, for example, is not going to be easily – if ever – repaired. But identifying the pain which is compelling us to eat may help us see that eating, too, isn't going to make our sadness go away. We can come to see that food is cold comfort at best.

Sometimes, however, clarification opens up the possibility of creative compromise with the failure of our lives to engage us. We may indeed find solutions, albeit not the ones we would have foreseen. These solutions may have to do with taking a chance on that open-ended future that has in the past filled us with such trepidation that we found ourselves stuck in the past, repeating unsatisfactory defenses (like eating), and making ourselves even more miserable.

NOTHING SUCCEEDS LIKE FAILURE, NOTHING FAILS LIKE SUCCESS

When we don't do something in the present because we are convinced that we are not going to succeed, what we are really doing is ensuring our failure by bringing the imagined future

Chapter Five

into the present moment. For some reason we prefer a known failure to the risk of being surprised by the future – perhaps being disappointed by it, but perhaps not!

The real problem isn't experiencing failure, because regaining the weight we've already lost would also be a failure. This is so, not because there is some ideal weight human beings have to be, but rather because *we* decided we didn't want to be holding on to this weight. Like losing weight, maintaining our weight loss is a *choice* we have to make. It is something we have to decide we want enough to do it instead of something else: namely, eating again to excess.

Making sure that we fail takes away the threat of disappointment. And for some reason, disappointment is for some people more painful than failure. Perhaps this is because disappointment incorporates the idea that we have entertained an expectation or hope or desire. We've opened ourselves up to something, and that may make us feel vulnerable and exposed.

To confront change requires courage. To confront the unknown requires even more. It requires faith: faith that you are going to be able to handle whatever the future may bring, including failure.

Here's an exercise that can help you step into the future.

IMAGINAL EXERCISE #37
MY GUARDIAN ANGEL

Closing your eyes and breathing out three times, imagine that you have called your guardian angel down from the heavens to stand before you. Breathe out.

Exchange every part of yourself, externally and internally, that you wish to change, with your guardian angel. Thank your guardian angel for always being available to you.

Breathe out and hear your angel saying: "Fear not, for what you fear never was and never will be."

Breathe out and open your eyes.

THE FEAR OF SELF-TRANSFORMATION

Sometimes we prefer repeating past failures rather than opening up to future possibilities (including disappointment) because what is familiar is usually easier to cope with than what is unfamiliar. You know yourself in the present in a certain way, even with your inadequacies. You have accepted that this is who you are. You worry that if you were to change, your world would change, and you wouldn't know yourself or your world. Perhaps you worry that you might virtually disappear were you

Chapter Five

to remain thin. Perhaps you experience your weight as securing your place in the world, making you present and visible, making you matter. Perhaps you fear that were you to maintain your weight loss you might become insignificant.

As with all our excuses we are reprocessing the grounds for our having gained weight in the first place. Perhaps when our mothers and fathers insisted we eat three meals a day and finish everything on our plates or when the school health teacher wedded our idea of eating to the food pyramid, bottom heavy with carbohydrates, we came to believe that with anything less than a lot of everything we just wouldn't survive. And so we ate and ate and ate, and will eat again.

Sometimes it's useful to return to our early experiences of eating and identify the features of those experiences.

IMAGINAL EXERCISE #38
THE DINNER TABLE OF CHILDHOOD

Closing your eyes and breathing out three times, see yourself seated at the table of your childhood. See who is there with you. Know how you feel at the table. Look at each one at the table. Recall how you feel about them. Bring the taste of this experience into the present. Breathe out and open your eyes, bringing that taste with you.

One man in our group, when he returned to the table of his youth, recalled how important it was to his mother that he eat all the food on his plate. He ate in order to be a "good boy" and thereby secure his place in his mother's affection. By eating seconds, i.e., by overeating, he imagined he might receive even more love.

For another member of our group the childhood memory was quite different. Returning to her childhood table, this young woman found herself in her high chair with a bowl of oatmeal in front of her on her tray. Her parents and brother were blurred in the distance. She felt herself completely alone, not eating, and ignored by the rest of the family. When it was suggested to her that she now visualize herself at the family table a few years later, she found herself seated next to her father, still not interested in eating, and still completely ignored by the rest of the members of the family. Overeating had become, for this woman, a way to be noticed, recognized. Her large size protected her against these early childhood feelings of smallness and insignificance.

Sometimes body size is a dramatic way of declaring to other people: *here I am! I matter.* It is also a way of insisting that this is *who* we are, against the desire of other people to see us or define us differently. The only problem is that we make these

Chapter Five

statements at our own expense. We punish ourselves for other people's inability to see us as we would wish them to.

DANGEROUS BEAUTY

Body image is a complex phenomenon. While wanting to lose weight usually has to do with an ideal body image we wish to pursue, nonetheless the body we have, and have had for so many years, is integrally a part of who we are and how we experience ourselves. Yielding some of that mass can seem literally endangering. It might make us feel vulnerable to whatever forces the weight we were holding on to protected us against.

The question each of us must ask ourselves is: do I really need to be weighted down this way?

> *One woman who had already lost 50 pounds but wished to lose another 20 found that, no matter what she did, she could not lose the additional weight. Through bringing her reasons for eating and her anxieties concerning the future into focus, she was able to see that she was guarding against the possibility of her own vulnerability, were she to attain the body size she desired. She was then able to work on building up her sense of self-confidence so as to confront the world on her own (new) terms.*

This problem was brought into even sharper relief by another beautiful young woman with 20 pounds to lose who argued that, while she would like to be slimmer, her high-powered executive job required that she be taken seriously. For her, slimness was for movie stars and models. It is what made them sexually, rather than intellectually, attractive to men. And indeed, when this woman did lose the weight, she found herself the subject of a considerable amount of new male interest. This is what she had feared. It was also, however, what she learned to manage, without in any way damaging her image as a corporate executive.

For many women feelings of vulnerability have to do with their sexuality. They fear the sexual advances that might be made towards them. Or they fear their own sexual desire. Overeating is one way women and men deal with their sexual feelings. By overeating, they make themselves unattractive. Not only do they then have less to fear from the sexual desires of others, but they have a ready excuse for why others do not find them sexually attractive. And, in the process, they are also able to block their own feelings of sexual desire and repress any fears they might have. The body becomes not sexually desirable and, often, not sexually desiring.

It is a general rule of the psychological life that it is better to acknowledge feelings than to repress or deny them. We cannot

Chapter Five

control our feelings. We can control our behavior, which is to say, what we do with our feelings. We can also learn how to say "no" to the feelings of others in some way other than displaying that answer as a layer of body fat. Review Imaginal Exercise #13 in chapter 4 on Saying No. "No" is a perfectly legitimate response in certain situations, and we should learn to say it.

Even for married people, unresolved feelings concerning their sexual attractiveness can become a reason for overeating. Perhaps they need to guard themselves against becoming attracted to or becoming the object of attraction in relation to other men or women. Or perhaps they somehow do not know how to handle what they experience as the excessive demands of the bedroom. Whatever the conflict, it is important to discover the source of your feelings and find some other, less self-destructive way of responding to them.

THE ANXIETY OF REGRET

Another reason we might have for regaining the weight we have lost is the fear that, achieving the slenderness we desired, we might experience pangs of regret for all those years when we weren't thin. How hard it may be to face all those missed opportunities: the outfit we couldn't buy when we were 20, the man or woman we didn't attract at 25, the self-confidence we lacked at 30 and the job we didn't get at 35…

Just as we can slash our way fearlessly into the future, so we can unburden ourselves of the past.

This exercise may help:

IMAGINAL EXERCISE #39
DISCARDING THE PAST

Closing your eyes and breathing out three times, imagine yourself with a heavy, oversized backpack on your back. It contains all your past regrets, all your disappointments. Make a mental list of its contents. Identify the burdens you are carrying.

Find yourself in front of a staircase and begin to climb the steps.

Now, hear and know that your burdens are one by one falling from your backpack. Feel the pack getting lighter. When it's empty, throw the bag away as well.

When you reach the top of the stairs, feel yourself lighter, taller, and unburdened. Keep this feeling for yourself.

Breathe out and open your eyes.

Chapter Five

THE BEAUTIFUL ME

As we become adults it seems necessary to accept certain things about ourselves. But realism and rationality can become rationalizations and defenses. Even if we feel ourselves not to be beautiful or handsome enough, we are likely to take some steps in the direction of beauty: go to the beauty parlor or barber shop, use cosmetics, buy a dress or hat or new suit we think is flattering, and so on and so forth. We accept we aren't beautiful or handsome, but we do something about it.

You no longer need to accept that you have no choice but to be fat. You no longer have to counteract in advance your potential disappointment in the new outfit or the new hairdo or the new figure. You no longer need to use weight to punish yourself, or to protect yourself, or act out your relationship to the world through food.

Beauty, we all know, is in the eyes of the beholder. We are our own best beholders. When we acknowledge our uniqueness and inner beauty, we make it visible to the outside world. Our souls, our internal selves, come to be reflected in our eyes. There is no such thing as not being beautiful enough. We make ourselves beautiful when we believe in our beauty.

Once it was easier to stay an ugly duckling than to discover you were a swan. Once it was easier not to let your inner beauty out. No longer.

Being beautiful isn't about taking the easy path. It is about taking the path of your desire. It is about accepting the radiance of yourself.

IMAGINAL EXERCISE #40
THE FLOWER GARDEN

Closing your eyes and breathing out three times, imagine that you are in a flower garden. See the first flower in front of you. Notice its color, its shape. Inhale its aroma. Now see the second flower, and know it, its color, shape, and smell. Now see still another flower and come to know it in the same way.

Imagine yourself becoming the first flower. Feel its essence as it opens to the sun. Becoming yourself again, imagine yourself as the second flower. And now the third, each time feeling the essence of the flower, as it opens to the sun.

Knowing the essential being of these three flowers, decide which one is you. Become that flower. Feel its being becoming your own. Now returning to yourself and sensing the flower within you, breathe out and open your eyes, transformed.

Chapter Five

THE LIGHTNESS OF BEING

One of the things our weight covered over was our reluctance to deal with the things that our weight covered over. Being fat was for many of us an excuse for not getting the things we desired and feared we couldn't have: marriage, fame, fortune – the works. There was a reason for my sadness, you said to yourself, and there is absolutely nothing I can do about it. I am fat. But what you have discovered by dieting was that there was something you could do about it. Once, your body was a good place in which to hide. But now you have come out of hiding. You are ready to discover what possibilities life holds for you.

Perhaps a way to look at ourselves is that for every pound of excess weight we once carried there was an empty space being filled in with fat. Perhaps we need to ask those empty spaces whether they need to be filled in and weighted down. Perhaps we need to ask them if they aren't willing to remain empty for a while: to wait and see what the future might bring.

IMAGINAL EXERCISE #41
HEART TO HEART

Breathing out one time, imagine yourself turning your senses inward to your center. Feel inside your body, sense your arms and your shoulders, your chest, your stomach, your back, your neck, your legs. Focus now on your stomach. Ask your guts, now, what are they feeling? What emotion is hidden there inside your stomach? Is there an emptiness within that is crying out to you? What truth will fill your emptiness? Hear the answers to your questions.

Breathe out.

Now look into your chest and find your heart.

Ask your heart what it is asking for.

Ask your heart what is hidden within it. What love is it feeling? What pain is it suffering?

If there is any pain, see and know how to heal your heart's discomfort with the warmth of golden light. Feel your heart beating perfectly.

Breathe out and open your eyes.

Consider what you experienced in the exercise and what you now understand about the emptiness you were feeling.

How else might you address these issues? What else might you do in your life to satisfy the emotions that are in the pit of your stomach?

Does the empty space require filling? Might you leave it empty?

Chapter Five

IMAGINAL EXERCISE #42
KNOWING YOURSELF

Closing your eyes and breathing out three times, go to the place of emptiness that you feel inside your body. See how it looks. Ask what the emptiness truly wants. Ask if food is the only substance that can satisfy the feeling. Now, ask what purpose the feeling of emptiness serves in your life. Ask how it helps you to be who and what you are. Know the truth of what you are. Hear that truth from the inside of your body. Breathe out and open your eyes, bringing new understanding with you.

When you interrogate your empty spaces, you may find that you have no choice but to fill them. They are that painful. Listen to their demands. Find ways, other than eating, to satisfy them.

But perhaps you will discover that your empty spaces are good friends and allies. Perhaps they are holding open places of choice and possibility.

If you are able to keep from filling them in with everything and anything that comes to mouth, you will find that the empty spaces are capable of buoying you up, letting you sail into the future.

IMAGINAL EXERCISE #45
THE BUTTERFLY

Closing your eyes and breathing out three times, imagine that you are a caterpillar, in a cocoon, on a branch of a tree. Sense how secure and comfortable you feel in this dark, protected place. You feel you could stay here forever.

Breathe out. Feel the life force within you stirring. Know that you are slowly transforming into a butterfly. Feel your colorful wings sprouting on your back.

Breathe out. Sense now that the time is approaching for you to emerge.

See the cocoon slowly opening around you. Feel the warmth of the sun, shining in and lighting up your world. Feel your bright, colorful wings unfolding. Know your own beauty. Know you are now able to fly.

Breathe out and open your eyes.

Perhaps your empty spaces aren't empty spaces at all. Perhaps they are spaces of lightness and grace, ready to illuminate your life and lift you up. Wouldn't it be nice to discover that you have wings and can fly?

Appendix:
Our Soup-er Recipes

BLENDED ZUCCHINI SOUP

You won't believe this soup doesn't have a single potato in it!

Ingredients:
- 6 zucchinis
- 1 medium-size onion
- 2 cloves of garlic
- 1 teaspoon mild curry paste or 2 tablespoons curry powder
- 2 tablespoons low-fat seasoned broth
- handful of dill

Preparation:
- Slice the onion and garlic into a saucepan.
- Cover with water and seasoned broth.
- Heat over a low flame for 3 minutes.
- Add sliced zucchini.

- Add enough water to cover all the soup ingredients.
- Add curry paste or powder.
- Cook on a low flame for 30 minutes, or until the zucchini is soft.
- With the flame off, add the fresh dill.
- Allow the soup to cool and blend until smooth. The soup can be garnished with chives or scallion greens.

The soup can be served hot or cold, and the cold soup can be topped with a spoonful of yogurt.

Feel free to experiment with this recipe. Add a few carrots along with the zucchini, or more onion and garlic. Add parsley along with the dill. Use carrots instead of zucchini, spice with marjoram, and top off with yogurt. Use different low-fat broths: chicken-flavored, beef-flavored, vegetable, etc. Or mix a bunch of vegetables: carrots, string beans, zucchinis, onions, celery, and leave unblended.

This is a soup of a multitude of possibilities, and a variety of satisfactions. Enjoy.

Appendix

CABBAGE SOUP

This is an old dieting favorite. It can be eaten for two to three days to jump-start a diet (as Susan Estrich recommends in *Making the Case for Yourself*) or to dislodge a stalled one.

Ingredients:
- 1 head of red or white cabbage
- 1 medium-size onion
- 3 cloves garlic
- 1 stalk celery
- 12 fresh mushrooms, sliced
- 1 green pepper
- 2 carrots
- string beans, 1 package frozen or 8 oz. fresh
- 28-oz. can fat-free canned tomatoes, with liquid
- parsley or dill or cilantro
- 2 tablespoons low-fat seasoned broth
- salt and pepper

Preparation:
- Slice the vegetables into chunk-size pieces. Place in pot.
- Add tomatoes and liquid.
- Add water until the vegetables are covered.
- Season with low-fat broth.

- Cook for 1 hour on a slow flame or until all the vegetables are soft.
- Season with salt and pepper to taste.
- Add parsley, dill, or cilantro after the soup has cooked.

This soup can be frozen and saved for a quick meal. It can be blended as well, for a different eating experience. A handful of raisins and a bit of artificial sweetener can be added to produce a stuffed-cabbage taste!

Some people have preferred this soup without the tomatoes. Either way, it's delicious. Experiment!

Appendix

CAULIFLOWER SOUP

This soup tastes like vichyssoise, without the calories!

Ingredients:
- 1 cauliflower, washed and cut into chunks or broken into florets
- 1 onion
- 3 cloves garlic
- 1 leek, thinly sliced
- 2 tablespoons low-fat seasoned broth
- chives or scallion greens to garnish

Preparation:
- Slice the onion and garlic into a saucepan.
- Cover with water and seasoned broth.
- Heat over flame for 3 minutes.
- Add the cauliflower and leek.
- Cover the vegetables with water and cook for approximately 20 minutes, or until the cauliflower is soft.
- Allow the soup to cool and blend until smooth.

Serve the soup hot or cold. Garnish with chives or scallion greens. It's incredibly delicious.

PEPPER SOUP – RED OR YELLOW

The difference is in the parsley and basil.

Ingredients:
- 6 peppers, cleaned and sliced
- 1 onion
- 3 cloves of garlic
- 2 tablespoons low-fat seasoned broth
- 1 teaspoon mild curry paste or 2 tablespoons curry powder
- handful of chopped parsley or basil (for the red pepper soup, only)

Preparation:
- Slice the onion and garlic into a saucepan.
- Cover with water and seasoned broth.
- Heat over low flame for 3 minutes.
- Add sliced peppers.
- Add enough water to cover all the ingredients.
- Add curry.
- Cook on a low flame for 30 minutes, or until the peppers are soft.
- Allow the soup to cool.
- *Before* blending the soup, remove three cups of liquid and put aside.

Appendix

- Blend the peppers until smooth, adding the removed liquid as necessary to produce the desired consistency.
- For the **red pepper soup** only, add chopped parsley as a garnish.

The red soup is rich and sensuous. The yellow soup is a surprise splash of color.

Index of Imaginal Exercises

#1 A Room of Your Own (Introductory Exercise) 51
#2 The Two Mirrors 57
#3 The Obstacle in the Path 60
#4 Holding On 64
#5 Repairing the Weave 67
#6 My Time 78
#7 Fixing the Clock 80
#8 Drawing the Curtain 82
#9 Setting the Date 83
#10 Thankfulness and Appreciation 87
#11 The Zipper 88
#12 The Photo 89
#13 Saying No 93
#14 Mindfulness 96
#15 The Other Side of the Mirror 98
#16 The Moment After 100
#17 The Inner Truth 101
#18 The Internal Menu 104
#19 The Milky Way 113
#20 The Body Overhaul 114

#21	Slimming Down	127
#22	A Quiet Cleansing	130
#23	Rolling Back	134
#24	Au Revoir to the Past	136
#25	Breaking the Cycle	140
#26	Through the Eye of the Needle	144
#27	The Energizing Sprint	152
#28	Be Your Own Hero	157
#29	Knowing What You Need	163
#30	Knowing the Truth	165
#31	Magnifying and Erasing the Habit	168
#32	Three Doors	169
#33	Through a Veiled Window	175
#34	Boredom and Its Discontents	178
#35	Vanishing the Fear of Overeating	184
#36	A Question of Interest	187
#37	My Guardian Angel	190
#38	The Dinner Table of Childhood	191
#39	Discarding the Past	196
#40	The Flower Garden	198
#41	Heart to Heart	199
#42	Knowing Yourself	201
#43	The Butterfly	202

www.ingramcontent.com/pod-product-compliance
Lightning Source LLC
Chambersburg PA
CBHW070849050426
42453CB00012B/2094